Asian Co

Two Cookbooks in one, Japanese Ramen Cookbook & Korean Cookbook with more than 180 Recipes to cook at home

Table of Contents

Ramen Cookbook 10

Introduction.. 11

Toppings... 12

Flavors and Soup Types 16

Pork Ramen Recipes 19

Basic Pork Ramen.. 19

Lazy Sunday Spicy Pork Ramen 21

Low-Cal Pork Ramen 24

Ramen with Braised Pork.. 25

Keto Pork Ramen... 27

Whole Wheat Pork Ramen 29

Pork Ramen with Turnips.. 30

Ramen with Pork Cutlets 32

Miso Pork Ramen 34

Slow Cooker Ramen with Pork 36

Spicy Keto Ramen Bowl 38

Shoyu Ramen 39

Chicken Ramen Recipes 43

Basic Low Sodium Chicken Ramen 43

Chicken Ramen.. 45

Ramen With Chicken Nuggets 47

Spicy Chicken Ramen.. 49

Miso Chicken Ramen 52

Rotisserie Chicken Ramen... 53

Hearty Chicken Breast Ramen 55

Spicy Chicken Ramen Version 2.. 57

Slow Cooker Chicken Ramen.. 59

Big Bowl Chicken Ramen 61

Chicken Ramen with Brown Sugar 63

Chicken and Veggie Ramen 64

Chicken Ramen With Spicy Peanut Sauce.................................... 66

Work Week Chicken Ramen... 68

Sesame Chicken Salad Ramen 70

Low-Cal Chicken Ramen 72

Low Carb Keto Chicken Ramen 73

Ramen Noodles with Canned Chicken.. 75

Beef Ramen Recipes 77

Ramen Noodles with Mongolian Beef 77
Ramen with Beef and Broccoli 79
Low-Cal Beef Ramen 80
Spicy Beef Ramen Soup 81
Ground Beef Ramen Skillet 82
Oriental Beef Ramen Noodles 83
Ramen Mason Jars 85
Crock Pot Beef Ramen 86
Spicy Beef Ramen Chashu 88
Easy Weekday Ramen 90
Ramen Veggie Skillet 91
Beef and Garlic Ramen 92
Keto Beef Ramen Bowl 94
Spicy Keto Beef Ramen 96
Ramen with Bison 98

Seafood Ramen Recipes 99

Crockpot Seafood Ramen 99
Ramen with Chicken and Shrimp 101
Creamy Tuna Ramen Noodles 103
Simple Shrimp Ramen 104
Low-Cal Seafood Ramen 105
Shrimp Pho Ramen Soup 106
Shrimp Ramen Stir Fry 108
Kimchi Seafood Ramen 110
Shrimp and Broccoli Ramen 112
Seafood Ramen Mix 113
Spicy Salmon Ramen 114
Crab and Veggie Ramen 116
Salmon and Veggie Ramen Noodles 117
Keto Shrimp Ramen with Shirataki Noodles 119
Shiitake Shrimp Bowl with Cabbage and Sriracha 120

Vegetarian Ramen Recipes 122

Simple Vegan Ramen Noodles 122
Spicy Garlic Tofu Ramen 124
Creamy Ramen Noodles 126
Savory Vegetable Ramen 127
Ramen with Spring Peas and Mushrooms 130
Veggie Ramen with Tofu 132
Fried Egg Ramen 133

4

Everyday Vegetarian Ramen Bowl *134*
Sweet Potato Ramen *136*
Turmeric Vegetarian Ramen Bowl *138*
Vegan Ramen *139*
Miso Coconut Vegan Ramen *141*
Herb and Veggie Ramen *143*
Ramen Veggie Skillet *144*
Low-Cal Veggie Ramen *145*

Vegetarian Ramen Mason Jars **146**
Ramen with Cauliflower and Pine Nuts *148*
Ramen with Almond Butter *149*

Gluten Free Ramen Recipes **151**
Chicken Rice Noodle Ramen *151*
Beef Rice Noodle Ramen *153*
Quick Gluten Free Ramen *154*
No Noodle Soup *155*
Veggie Noodle Chicken Ramen *156*
Sriracha Non- Gluten Ramen Dish *158*
Gluten Free Sesame Garlic Ramen *160*
Shirataki Ramen *161*

Homemade Noodle Recipes **163**
Homestyle Egg Noodles *163*

Ramen Sides Recipes **167**
Ramen Wraps *167*
Ramen Trail Mix *169*
Ramen Coleslaw *170*
Instant Pot Soft Boiled Eggs *171*
Black Bean Ramen Pilaf *173*
Corn and Basil Feta Slaw *174*
Pickled Cucumbers *175*
Tamagoyaki (Rolled Omelette) *177*
Onigiri (Rice Ball) *179*
Kinpira Gobo *181*
Boiled Squid in a Miso Vinaigrette *183*

Conclusion **184**
Korean Cookbook **185**
Introduction **188**

Introduction to Korean Cuisine **189**

Location: Where Korean Cooking Comes From 189
Yin and Yang: A Philosophy of Balance 192
Five Elements: Harmony of Flavors 194

The Korean Pantry **195**

Gochugaru (Korean Chili Powder) 195
Gochujang (Korean Chili Paste) 196
Method 196
Doenjang (Fermented Soybean Paste) 196
Ganjang (Soy Sauce) 197
Chamgireum (Toasted Sesame Oil) 197
Aekjeot (Fish Sauce) 197
Cheongju (Rice Wine) 197
Ssalsikcho (Rice Wine Vinegar) 198
Kkae (Toasted Sesame Seeds) 198
Chapsal (Glutinous or Sweet Rice Flour) 198

Korean Kitchen Tools **199**

Dolsot (Stone Bowl) 199
Onggi (Clay Pot) 199
Siru (Earthenware Steamer) 200
Sujeo (Utensils) 200
Tabletop Grill 201
Rice Cooker 202

Korean Staples: Recipes & Guidelines for Common Dishes **203**

Bap (Rice) 203
Gukbap (Rice Soup) 205
Juk (Rice Porridge) 207
Bokkeum-bap (Fried Rice 1) 208
Mushroom Rice 210
Bibimbap (Rice Dish with Meat and Vegetables) 212
Tteok-bokki (Spicy Rice Cakes) 215
BibimGuksu (Spicy Noodle Dish) 217
Japchae (Glass Noodle Stir Fry) 219
MulNaengmyeon (Cold Noodle Soup) 221
Mandu (Dumplings 1) 223
Kimchi Mandu (Dumplings 2) 227
Bulgogi (Grilled Beef) 228
Bulgogi Sauce 230
Daweaji Bulgogi (Grilled Pork) 231

6

Dak Bulgogi (Grilled Chicken 1)...233
Dak Bulgogi (Grilled Chicken 2)...235
Galbi (Grilled Short Ribs)...237
Mulgogi Gochujang (Spicy Fish)...239
Kkanpung Saeu (Spicy and Sweet Shrimp) 240

Banchan: Shared Small Dishes for Every Meal **242**

Hobak Bokkeum (Stir-fried Zucchini)..243
Oi Bokkeum (Stir-fried cucumbers) 245
Gaji Bokkeum (Stir-fried Eggplant) 246
Myulchi Bokkeum (Stir-fried Anchovies) 248

Buchimgaeor Jeon (Korean Pancakes) 249
Kimchi Buchimgae (Kimchi Pancake)...249
Pajeon (Scallion Pancake) 251
Hobak Buchimgae (Zucchini Pancakes) 253
Gamja Jeon (Potato Pancakes)..255
Pancake Dipping Sauce 257

Namul (Vegetables)..258
Kongnamul Muchim (Seasoned Bean Sprouts)....................................259
Sigeumchi Namul (Blanched Spinach) 260
Gaji Namul (Steamed Eggplant) 261
Watercress Namul 262
Mu Namul (Stir-fried Radish) 263

Other Banchan 265
Kongjang (Dried Beans in Soy) 266
Gamja Jorim (Braised Potatoes) 267
Dubu Jorim (Braised Tofu) 269
Oi Muchim (Cucumber Salad) 269
Mu Saengchae (Spicy Radish Salad) 271
Putbaechu Doenjang Muchim (Soybean Paste Cabbage) 272
Goguma Mattang (Candied Sweet Potatoes) 273
Soy Sauce Eggs 274
GimGui (Toasted Seaweed)...275
Ssamjang (Dipping Sauce) 277

Kimchi and Other Pickles..**278**

Kimchi 278
Traditional Cabbage Kimchi 278

Quick Kimchi..281
Kkaekdugi (Radish Kimchi)...283
Baek-kimchi (Chili free Kimchi or "White Kimchi")...............................284

Dongkimchi (Winter Kimchi) 286

Nabak-kimchi (Spring Kimchi) 288

Oisobagi (Cucumber Kimchi) 289

Pakimchi (Scallion Kimchi).. 290

Kkaennip Kimchi (Perilla Leaf Kimchi) 291

Jangajii.. 291

Soy Sauce Pickles 292

Doenjang (Soybean) Pickles 293

Brined Pickles 294

Jjeotgal.. 295

Soups & Stews **296**

Kimchi KongnamulGuk (Kimchi & Bean Sprout Soup) 297

Baechu Doengjang Guk (Cabbage Soup with Soybean Paste)........... 299

Ganjaguk (Potato Soup).. 301

Tteokguk (Rice Cake Soup) 303

Oi Naengguk (Cold Cucumber Soup)..................................... 305

Dak Gomtang (Chicken Soup).. 306

Yukgaejang (Spicy Beef and Vegetable Soup)......................... 308

Galbitang (Beef Short Rib Soup)... 310

Haemul Jeongol (Seafood Hot Pot)....................................... 312

Bulgogi Jeongol (Beef Hot Pot).. 314

Kimchi Jjigae (Kimchi Stew).. 316

Haemul Sundubu Jjigae (Seafood and Tofu Stew).................. 318

Hobak Gochujang Jjigae (Spicy Zucchini Stew) 320

Budae Jjigae (Army Stew)... 322

Saewoojuk (Shrimp and Rice Porridge)................................. 324

Desserts: Hangwa and Tteok **326**

Hangwa 326

Dasik (Tea Cookies) 326

Green Tea Cookies 326

Variation: Berry Tea Cookies 327

Gwapyeon (Fruit Jelly).. 328

Jeonggwa (Fruit Jerky).. 330

Yaksik (Sweet Rice with Nuts and Fruit).............................. 332

Yugwa (Sweet Rice Crackers)... 334

Yumil-gwa (Fried Dough Sweet) 336

Kkultarae (King's Candy).. 338

Yeot-gangjeong (Sesame Candy) 340

Tteok..**341**

Steamed Tteok 342
   Kongtteok (Bean tteok)..342
   Jeungpyeon (Rice wine tteok) 343
   Baekseolgi (Raisin tteok) 345

Pounded Tteok 346
   Injeolmi (Sweet Beantteok) 346
   Kkaeinjeolmi (Black Sesame tteok) 348
   Danpatjuk (Sweet Bean & Rice Dumpling Soup)....................349

Shaped Tteok 351
   Songpyeon (Half-moon stuffed tteok).....................................351
   Baram Tteok (Round stuffed tteok)..353

Pan Fried Tteok 354
   Hwajeon (Flower tteok) 354
   Bukkumi (Filled Crescent tteok) 355

Drinks **356**

Cha (Tea).. 356
   Green Tea: How to Brew...356
   Barley Tea: How to Brew 357
   Fruit Teas: How to Brew 357
   Cinnamon Tea 358

Non-Alcoholic Drinks 358
   Sujeonggwa (Cinnamon Ginger Punch) 358
   Subak Hwachae (Watermelon Punch)....................................358
   Sikhye (Sweet Rice Drink) 359

Alcoholic Drinks.. 360
   Soju Yogurt Cocktail...361
   Flavored Liquors 361
   Ginger Cocktail 361

Conclusion **362**

Ramen Cookbook

*100 Quick and Easy Ramen Recipes to Prepare At Home,
Step By Step Explained,
with Traditional Toppings and Flavors*

Introduction

Ramen originated as a Chinese dish that was adopted by Japan then further integrated into American culture. It was first brought to Japan by Chinese immigrants during the late 19th century and has since come a long way from its humble origins.

Today, ramen is a well-known entity and if you haven't eaten Ramen you have almost certainly heard of the dish. In Japan, it could be said that ramen is much like the American hamburger, as it is convenient, inexpensive, and widely accessible. Just like almost anything though, the quality of ramen can vary depending on where you are. In the U.S. things are a little bit different. The accessibility of ramen is still there, however, the quality is often not as impressive unless you live in a dense city where those who specialize in the cooking and preparation of ramen primarily exist. Outside of these speciality chefs, one is usually left with only popular instant ramen substitutes.Once again, while far reaching, these instant ramen substitutes offer only a small reflection of the rich and complex flavors offered by more traditional and fresh ramen recipes. Not only that, but the nutritional benefits of ramen are often lost in the preparation of easy instant ramen. Some researchers have concluded that consuming instant ramen more than once or twice a week can increase the risk of developing diabetes, heart disease and/or stroke. This is bad news for the average struggling college student. There is, however, an alternative. Homemade ramen is, more nutritious, healthier, tastes better, and can be an easy and enjoyable experience both in its creation and consumption. It is also a very versatile dish, being able to be changed and used in any way the creator desires. You can still have the ease of using instant noodles, but with just a bit more effort you can upgrade your experience.

This book will give you the recipes needed to make ramen your own. It will go over the bases for the different broths you can use, the noodle types, toppings, and of course, easy and straightforward recipes that will almost certainly become staples in your weekly meal planning, ranging from the quick, the easy and the quick and easy.

Toppings

Toppings Ramen is a fun dish. Part of its appeal is the amount of toppings that can add to the experience. Here is a small list of ramen toppings, but the possibilities are actually endless. Experiment with different combinations and visit asian grocery stores to find more specialized ingredients.

- **Bean Sprouts**: High in fiber, fatty acids, antioxidants and vitamin A, these ancient sprouts can be eaten frozen fresh or canned.

- **Black Garlic Oil**: Is a black oil that is rich in amino acids and allicin. It has double the antioxidants of its white garlic counterpart.

- **Carrots**: typically prepared in many different ways, this vegetable is actually a colored root and is full of vitamins, like vitamin A from beta-carotene, vitamin K and B6.

- **Eggs**: A very versatile protein which can easily be incorporated into any ramen dish. Great soft boiled but can also be broken right into the cooking soup.

- **Fancy Tubesteaks**: another way to say sausage. Typically a Japanese reference.

- **Fermented Red Pepper Paste**: Also referred to as Gochujang, it adds depth, flavor and spice to dishes. Particularly use in Korean cooking.

- **Fried Onions**: Crispy onion pieces. Can be bought pre made, or made at home.

- **Fried String Potatoes**: A crunchy potato option of thinly sliced pieces.

- **Furikake**: a special Japanese seasoning that is added to the top of cooked foods. Usually has a mix in it of sugar, salt, dried fish, sesame seeds, chopped seaweed, and MSG.

- **Garlic Chips**: thinly cut potato pieces flavored with garlic and deep fried or bakes.

- **Ginger**: an old cure all and anti-inflammatory food that adds pungent flavor to meats, veggies, and soups.

- **Green Onion**: a young onion that has a milder flavor than mature onions yet a little stronger than chives. Can be cooked or served raw.

- **Hot Sauce**: a spicy sauce, usually a blend of peppers and other ingredients.

- **Japanese Fish Cake**: processed seafood that's formed into loaves with distinctive patterns. Made with white fish.

- **Kimchi**: a fermented vegetable dish often made of a combination of cabbage, radish, onion, garlic, other veggies and seasoned. Has an abundance of vitamin A,B , and c, as well as, healthy bacteria.

- **Miso Butter**: miso is japanese seasoning made with fermented soybeans and koji. It becomes Miso Butter when combined with butter.

- **Miso Paste**: a thick paste made from fermented soybeans that is packed with umami flavor.

- **Mushrooms**: a fungal growth that comes in many varieties and is typically prepares in many different ways as well.

- **Parsley**: a flowering plant that is typically broken up and used to dress finished dishes. It adds balance to savory dishes. Can be used to reduce cancer risks, improve digestive tract and immune functions and reduce inflammation.

- **Pickled Ginger**: called amau shoga or gari in Japan, it is the fermented version of regular ginger.

- **Pork Belly**: not actually the stomach, but it is meat that runs along the underside of the pig. It has a lot of fat content that is very decadent and tender.

- **Red Pepper Flakes**: a seasoning comprised of dried red chilies that are crushed.

- **Roasted Garlic Butter**: butter infused with roasted garlic, adding a rich and savory flavor to any dish.

- **Rotisserie Chicken**: often found in most major grocery stores, this is a simple way to add flavor and protein to a dish without much extra effort.

- **Scallions**: actually just another name for green onions

- **Seasoned Bamboo Shoots**: also called menma, is a topping made from fermented bamboo shoots. They can be eaten alone but are often use as crunchy toppings.

- **Seaweed**: often referred to as roasted Nori, is a salty snack or topping that had high levels of calcium,and vitamins A and C.

- **Spinach**: a leafy vegetable that can easily be incorporated into nearly any dish. It provides vitamins A, C, and K and is a good source of iron and magnesium.

- **Sriracha Sauce**: a special hot sauce that is made from chili pepper paste and a mix of other spices.

- **Sweet Corn**: corn with a higher sugar content, resulting in extra sweetness. The result of a recessive mutation.

- **Tofu**: made of condensed soy milk and pressed into its iconic block shape.

- **Tubesteaks**: a fancy way of saying hot dog.

- **Umami**: a flavor that corresponds to the amino acid glutamate. It is used in seasonings to add an extra special dimension of flavor.

- **Yuzu Kosho**: a paste made from chiles fermented zest and salt.

Flavors and Soup Types

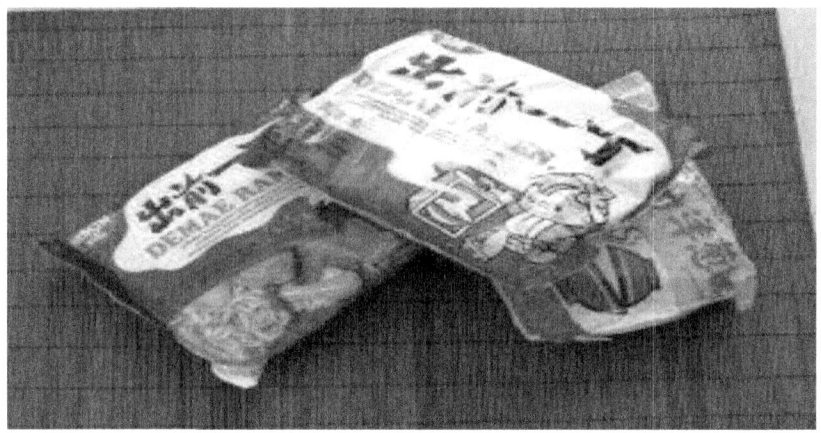

When approaching the topic of Ramen flavors there are two schools of thought. You can approach the subject from an instant ramen perspective or from a homemade broth point of view. The instant ramen add a specific flavor to bland water, while the broth or stock method brings together a melding of fluids. Broth is a more traditional method for creating a good ramn base. But instant flavorings can be an easy way to create a flavor you want or can't readily achieve by homemade means. This book will focus on the broth or stock based methods, however, it should be said that the instant ramen flavoring packs can be easily substituted into any traditional ramen recipe by using water instead and flavoring it with the appropriate amount of seasoning to taste or specifications. It can even be added to recipes listed in this book to boost certain flavors.

Maruchan Instant Ramen flavors:

- Beef
- Chicken
- Chicken Mushroom
- Chicken Tortilla
- Chili
- Creamy Chicken
- Lime Chili Shrimp
- Lime Shrimp
- Low Sodium Beef
- Low Sodium Chicken
- Oriental
- Picante Beef
- Picante Chicken
- Pork
- Roast Beef
- Roast Chicken
- Shrimp
- Sriracha Chicken
- Tonkotsu

It is important to note that while there are different flavors, there are also different types of broth. Here is a list of broth types to keep in mind when creating memorable dishes.

- **Miso Ramen**: if a broth uses fermented japanese soy pastes it is considered a miso broth ramen. They are usually very savory and full of flavor and this style can even be incorporated into other bowl types. These ramen tend to fall into the range of about 550 calories.

- **Shio Ramen**: This ramen is salt based. Typically light in color or clear, this is the most traditional method of preparing ramen. This style is often a bit saltier and fall around 400 calories in general.

- **Shoyu Ramen**: This ramen is a soy sauce based ramen. It is very common and pairs well with meats. The blend will vary. Typically around <u>475 calories</u>.

- **Tonkotsu Ramen**: This is a pork bone based broth. It is often the cloudiest base among its counterparts and combines aspects of both shio and shoyu, using both salt and soy sauce. This is the heaviest of all the soup bases in calories, ranging from around <u>600 calories</u>.

Let the information of the types of ramen inform you, however, it should not limit your creative process. As you can see, some types, like the tonkotsu ramen, utilizes other bowl qualities. Using these methods should only inform your thinking, not limit it.

Pork Ramen Recipes

Basic Pork Ramen

This recipe takes 30 mins to prep, 30 mins to cook and makes 4 servings.

- Protein: 24g
- Total Carbohydrate: 37g
- Total Fat: 8g
- Calories: 315

What to Use:

- Cilantro Leaves (.5 Cups)
- Halved and Thin Sliced Radishes (2)
- Large Grated Carrot (1)
- Soy Sauce (1 tbls)
- Ramen Noodles (2 packs)
- Low Sodium Chicken Broth (6 cups)
- Peeled and Sliced Ginger (2 inch piece)
- Sliced Scallions (8)
- Kosher Salt
- Black Pepper
- Boneless Pork Chops (2)
- Canola Oil (1 tbls)

What to Do:

- Dutch oven preferred but you can also just use a big pot.

- Heat oil over medium heat and place seasoned pork in pot to cook. Should take 2 to 3 mins. per side.

- Remove from heat and let rest for 5 mins. then slice thinly.

- Add ginger and scallions to the dutch oven. Cook for about 1 to 2 mins.

- Add broth and boil.

- Add noodles and cook for about 3 mins.

- Serve and top with carrots, radishes, sliced pork, cilantro and scallions.

Lazy Sunday Spicy Pork Ramen

This recipe takes 20 mins. prep, 4 hours and 40 mins to cook and makes 4 servings. It takes longer, but it's very easy to make. Perfect on a weekend or special occasion. Pork, can be substituted with Trader Joe's Fully Cooked Pork Belly.

- Protein: 45g
- Total Carbohydrate: 53g
- Total Fat: 30g
- Calories: 670

What to Use:

- Red Chili Flakes (1 tsp)
- Spring Onions (small bunch)
- Scallions (small bunch)
- Black Sesame Seeds (1 tsp)
- Sesame Seeds (1 tsp)
- Baby Spinach (3 cups)
- Sliced Leek (1)
- Ramen Noodles (7 oz)
- Eggs (4)
- Sliced Red Chili (1)
- Gochujang Paste (2 tbsp)
- Soy Sauce (3 tbsp)
- Mirin (2 tbsp)
- Chicken or Veggie Broth (8.5 cups)
- Chopped Ginger (thumb sized)
- Chopped Garlic Cloves (3)
- Celery Stalk (1)
- Onion (1)
- Peeled Carrots (2)
- Pepper
- Salt
- Rolled Pork Shoulder (2.2 lbs)

What to Do:

- Use a dutch oven or any other large pot that can be put in the oven. Preheat the oven to 300 while you prepare the pork.

- Season with salt and pepper to taste then place into the greased pot you will be using.

- Seal all sides of the pork.

- Remove the pork and place it to the side.

- Add into the pot onion, a whole carrot, garlic, celery, and ginger. Cook for 5 mins then add red Chili flakes, gochujang, soy sauce, stock, mirin and the sealed pork.

- Boil ingredients.

- Remove from heat and place pot into the oven.

- Leave in the oven for 4 hrs.

- Occasionally check on the pot and add boiling water if the water level falls.

- While that is happening, make the eggs.

- First make the eggs. Fill a large pot with water, enough to fully submerge both eggs. Take the eggs and boil them for 1 min. Then remove the eggs from the heat source and place to the side, covered, for an additional 8-10 mins. When the time has completed, drain the water and let both eggs cool before processing them to be incorporated into the dish.

- Remove the pot from the oven and remove the pork.

- Shred the pork.

- Strain the leftover liquid. Discard vegetables and debris.

- Put pork into the broth again and keep warm.

- Fry the leeks and season with salt and pepper.

- Prepare the noodles by boiling in water for 5 mins or as directed then rinsing them.

- Divy the noodles and leeks into bowls and pour the pork laden broth over them.

- Top with chili flakes, garnishes, peeled halved eggs, etc. and enjoy.

Low-Cal Pork Ramen

This recipe takes 5 mins to prep, 8 mins to cook and makes 1 serving.

- Protein: 5g
- Total Carbohydrates: 7g
- Total Fat: 1g
- Calories: 80

What to Use:

- Pepper (pinch)
- Ginger (pinch)
- Yeast Flakes (.25 tsp)
- Garlic Powder (.25 tsp)
- Garlic Salt (.25 tsp)
- Onion Powder (.5 tsp)
- Salt (1 tbls)
- Low Calorie Pork Broth (2 cups)
- Shirataki Noodles (1 package)

What to Do:

- Rinse and strain noodles.

- Add salt then continue rinsing.

- Pour pork broth into a large pot.

- Add noodles and bring the pot to a boil.

- Combine all your other ingredients, seasonings and yeast, into a bowl.

- Add seasonings to the pot when it begins to boil.

- Cook, stirring occasionally, for 3 mins.

Ramen with Braised Pork

This recipe takes 10 mins. to prep, 2 hrs. to cook and makes 6 servings.

- Protein: 22g
- Total Carbohydrate: 23g
- Total Fat: 16g
- Calories: 324

What to Use:

- Ramen Noodles Cooked (4 Oz)
- Cornstarch (2 tbls)
- Soy Sauce (2 tbls)
- Chicken Stock (8 cups)
- Vegetable Oil (2 tbls)
- Japanese Seven Spice (1 tsp)
- Firmly Packed Brown Sugar (2 tbls)
- Boneless Pork Shoulder (1 lb)

What to Do:

- Mix together the brown sugar and Japanese spices in a bowl, then rub the mix onto the pork. Let the pork rest in the fridge for and hour. You may also allow the pork to rest for up to 24 hours.

- When you are ready to prepare the meal, use a dutch oven.

- Heat oil within the dutch oven on medium high heat and sear the pork on all its sides.
- Add 4 cups stock to the pan then cook in the over for 2 hrs on 350.

- Remove the pork from the dutch oven and place to the side to rest.

- Add remaining broth to the dutch oven.

- Add cornstarch and soy sauce into a small bowl. Whisk the mixture into the dutch oven mix. Do so slowly.

- Bring the mix to a boil then add cooked noodles, sliced pork, and applicable toppings.

- Serve and enjoy.

Keto Pork Ramen

This recipe takes 30 mins to prep, 30 mins to make and creates 5 servings. It's great for those watching their carb intake.

- Protein: 21g
- Total Carbohydrate: 9g
- Total Fat: 20g
- Calories: 311

What to Use:

- Spiralized Zucchini (1)
- Beef Broth (6 cups)
- Fish Sauce (1 tbls)
- Apple Cider Vinegar (1 tbls)
- Coconut Aminos (.25 cups)
- Chopped Kale (3 cups)
- Ginger (1 tbls)
- Minced Garlic Cloves (4)
- Diced Green Onions (separate white parts) (4)
- Ground Pork (1 lb)

What to Do:

- In a large pot pour in oil and cook pork for about 6 to 7 mins.

- Add garlic, ginger, and white part of the green onions and cook for about 2 mins. stirring occasionally.

- Add coconut aminos, kale fish sauce, apple cider vinegar and beef broth.

- Bring to a boil.

- Reduce heat and add noodles. Cook until tender, about 3 mins.

- Serve and enjoy.

Whole Wheat Pork Ramen

This recipe takes 30 mins. to prep, 10 mins. to cook and makes 4 servings.

- Protein: 35g
- Total Carbohydrate: 47g
- Total Fat: 8g
- Calories: 400

What to Use:

- Thin Sliced Scallions (2)
- Cabbage and Carrot Slaw (2 cups)
- Whole Wheat Ramen Noodles or Spaghetti (8 oz)
- Reduced Sodium Soy Sauce (1.5 tsp)
- Pork Broth (3 cups)
- Eggs (4)

What to Do:
- First make the eggs. Fill a large pot with water, enough to fully submerge both eggs. Take the eggs and boil them for 1 min. Then remove the eggs from the heat source and place to the side, covered, for an additional 8-10 mins. When the time has completed, drain the water and let both eggs cool before processing them to be incorporated into the dish.

- In a big pot, add broth, soy sauce and 2 cups of water. Boil.
- Cook noodles according to directions on label.
- Drain noodles and add to individual bowls.
- Add veggies.
- Pour on broth.
- Dress with egg and scallions and any additional garnishes, like hot sauce or chile pepper flakes.

- Enjoy.

Pork Ramen with Turnips

This recipe takes 35 mins. to prep, 35 mins. to cook and makes 5 servings.

- Protein: 16g
- Total Carbohydrate: 15g
- Total Fat: 4g
- Calories: 160

What to Use:

- Baby Spinach (6 cups)
- Mushrooms (6 oz)
- Shao Hsing Rice Wine (1 tbls)
- Reduced Sodium Soy Sauce (1 tbls)
- White Miso (2 tbls)
- Water (3 cups)
- Low Sodium Chicken Broth (3 cups)
- Pork Tenderloin Pieces (8 oz)
- Minced Garlic Clove (1)
- Minced Ginger (1 tbls)
- Scallions (6)
- Peanut Oil (2 tsp.)
- Peeled Purple Top Turnips (1.5 lbs.)

What to Do:

- Spiralize turnips, about 10 cups.

- Heat oil in a big pot. Put in garlic, scallions and ginger and cook til fragrant.

- Add the pork, stirand brown

- Add broth, water, soy sauce, miso, and rice wine, then bring the mixture to a boil.

- Add noodles and cook for about 3 mins. Then serve.

- Dress with scallions and any additional garnishes, like hot sauce or chile pepper flakes.

- Enjoy.

Ramen with Pork Cutlets

This recipe takes 30 mins. prep, 41 mins to cook and makes 1 serving.

- Protein: 75.6g
- Total Carbohydrate: 90g
- Total Fat: 81.8g
- Calories: 1406

What to Use:

- Toppings: Black Pepper, Green Onion, Sushi Ginger (1 tbls), Tonkatsu Sauce (1 tbls)
- Miso Paste with Dashi (.5 tsp)
- Soy Sauce (1.75 tbls)
- Bonito Soup Stock (1.75 tbls)
- Shredded Dried Kombu (3 tbls)
- Instant Ramen Noodles (1 pack)
- Sage
- Basil
- Olive Oil (2 tbls)
- Boneless Pork Chop Slices (2)
- Spicy Sesame Oil (1.5 tsp)
- Egg (1)

What to Do:

- First make the egg. Fill a large pot with water, enough to fully submerge the egg. Take the egg and boil it for 1 min. Then remove the egg from the heat source and place to the side, covered, for an additional 8-10 mins. When the time has completed, drain the water and let it cool before processing it to be incorporated into the dish.

- Cover pork with half of the olive oil, sesame seeds, sage and basil to taste (generally just a bit).

- In a large skillet heat oil and cook the pork slices, 5 mins. on each side. Remove the pan from heat and let pork rest.

- Boil a large pot of water. Cook noodles for about 3 mins. or until tender. Then rinse them with water.

- Add noodles to a now empty pot and add the miso paste, soy sauce, bonito stock and kombu. Stir regularly. Takes about 3 to 5 mins.

- Move to a bowl and top with appropriate toppings to taste, garnish with peeled halved egg. Enjoy.

Miso Pork Ramen

This recipe takes 15 mins. prep, 15 mins. to make and creates 2 servings.

- Protein: 33g
- Total Carbohydrate: 129g
- Total Fat: 18g
- Calories: 797

What to Use:

- Water (2 cups)
- Ramen Noodle Packs (2) (or 5 Oz of fresh Ramen Chinese style noodles.)
- Sesame Oil (.5 teaspoons)
- Miso Paste (4 tbls)
- Soy Sauce (2 tsp)
- Sugar (1 tsp)
- Chicken Bouillon Powder (2 tsp)
- Warm Water (4 cups)
- Carrot Cut Thin (2 oz)
- Chopped Cabbage (4 oz)
- Bean Sprouts (5 oz)
- Ground Pork (2 oz)
- Minced Ginger (1 tsp)
- Garlic Clove (1)
- Canola Oil (1 tsp)

What to Do:

- In a skillet or wok heat oil. Add the garlic, ground pork and the ginger and cook until pork is done.

- Add veggies and cook til tender.

- Add water and bouillon powder. Stir, then add soy sauce and sugar. Bring to a boil.

- Reduce heat to a simmer and add miso making sure that it melds into the mixture.

- Add sesame oil.

- Remove from heat. Prepare noodles to the proper doneness according to packaging.

- Drain and present in individual bowls. Top with soup mixture.

- Enjoy.

Slow Cooker Ramen with Pork

This recipe takes 30 mins. prep, 8.5 hr. cook time and makes 6 servings. To lower cooking time considerably, use Trader Joe's pre cooked pork belly.

- Protein: 35g
- Total Carbohydrate: 29g
- Total Fat: 33g
- Calories: 560

What to Use:

- Toppings Cilantro, Sliced Jalapenos,
- Ramen Noodles (3 packets)
- Soy Sauce (3 tbls)
- Reduced Sodium Chicken Broth 32 oz (2)
- Chopped Garlic Cloves (6)
- Fine Chopped Ginger Root (2 tbls)
- Salt
- Sliced Green Onions, white and green separate (1 bunch)
- Sliced Cremini Mushrooms 8 oz (1 pkg)
- Boneless Pork Shoulder (fat trimmed) (6 cut sections)
- Vegetable Oil (2 tbls)

What to Do:

- Dutch oven preferred. Heat oil over medium high heat and cook half the pork for about 5 mins for each side. Cook all the pork this way, leaving finished pieces in a slow cooker.

- Cook on medium and add the oil that's left into the dutch oven. Cook veggies until soft. Then after 5 mins add the ginger and garlic. Cook till aromatic

- Store leftover green onions and ginger root in the fridge.

- Add broth to the mix. Scrape brown bits from the bottom of the pan as you stir then add the broth to the crock pot with the pork.

- Cook on low 10 hrs.

- Then bring pork to a cutting board or large plate and cut it into pieces. Remove excess fat if you'd like then place it back in the slow cooker.

- Stir in soy sauce and that remaining ginger root. Cover and cook for 15 to 20 mins.

- Prepare Ramen Noodles Separately and as advised.

- Drain and present in individual bowls. Top with soup mixture and remaining toppings. Enjoy.

Spicy Keto Ramen Bowl

This recipe takes 5 mins. to prep, 25 mins. to make and creates 5 servings.

- Protein: 12g
- Total Carbohydrate: 7g
- Total Fat: 3g
- Calories: 103

What to Use:

- Bone Broth (5 Cups)
- Shirataki Noodles (2 to 3 packets) or Zucchini Noodles
- Eggs (4)
- Mushrooms (4 oz)
- Rice Wine Vinegar (.25 Cups)
- Soy Sauce (.25 Cups)
- Fish Sauce (1 Tbls)
- Pepper (pinch)
- Salt (pinch)
- Chili Paste (1 Tsp)
- Minced Garlic Cloves (3)
- Grated Ginger (1 Tbls)
- Small Sliced Onion (1)
- Olive Oil (1 Tbls)

What to Do:

- Heat oil in a large pot. Cook onions for about 3 mins then add other ingredients, sans the egg of course.

- Simmer for 20 mins.

- Rinse noodles if from packaging, otherwise prepare as advised.

- Season broth to taste, add noodles.

- Serve and enjoy

Shoyu Ramen

This recipe takes 1 min prep, 3 mins. cook time and makes 6 servings.

- Protein: 57g
- Total Carbohydrate: 77g
- Total Fat: 34g
- Calories: 860

What to Use:

- Bonito Flakes (.25 Cups)
- Peeled and Sliced Ginger (1 inch)
- Head of Garlic (1)
- Peeled and Cut Carrots (2)
- Chopped Scallions (2 Bunches)
- Pork Spareribs (1 lb)
- Chicken Necks, Wings, or Backs (2 lbs)
- Vegetable Oil (2 Tbls)
- Kosher Salt
- Ground Black Pepper
- Boneless Pork Shoulder (1.5 lbs)
- Mirin (1 Tbls)
- Dry Sake (2 Tbls)
- Reduced Sodium Soy Sauce (.5 Cups)
- Dried Kombu Pieces (2)
- Chili Oil
- Toasted Sesame Oil
- Shichimi Togarashi
- Toasted Nori Sheets torn in half (3)
- Thin Sliced Scallions (6)
- Menma (.5 Cup)
- Dried Ramen Packages 3 oz (6)
- Eggs (3)

What to Do:

- Heat oil in a dutch oven, preferably. Cook pork shoulder and brown all over.

- Add the chicken, scallions, spareribs, ginger, garlic, and bonito flakes.

- Take the kombu from dashi and discard.

- Boil then reduce to a simmer. Skim the surface removing scum, skim and debris.

- Add the remaining dashi as the liquid in the pot begins to reduce.

- This will take about 2.5 to 3 hrs or until pork is tender.

- Remove pork and let it rest.

- Strain the stock mixture into a mesh strainer and remove the debris. (This includes chicken and ribs)

- To make the eggs, fill a large pot with water, enough to fully submerge the eggs. Take the eggs and boil for 1 min. Then remove the eggs from the heat source and place to the side, covered, for an additional 8-10 mins. When the time has completed, drain the water and let them cool before processing them to be incorporated into the dish.

- Slice pork thinly.

- Cook noodles separately in a large pot.

- Prepare Ramen Noodles as advised.

- Drain and present in individual bowls. Top with soup mixture and remaining toppings including the sliced pork. Garnish with peeled and halved eggs.
- Enjoy.

Pork Ramen

This recipe takes 5 hrs. It makes 4 servings. To lower cooking time considerably, use Trader Joe's pre cooked pork belly.

- Protein: 33g
- Total Carbohydrate: 50g
- Total Fat: 33g
- Calories: 636

What to Use:

- Ponzu (1 tbls)
- Peas (10 oz)
- Miso Paste (1 tbls)
- Low Sodium Pork Stock (6 cups)
- Dried Shiitakes (.5 oz)
- Bone in Shoulder Roast (2 lbs)
- Cooking Oil (1 tbls)
- Lime Wedges (1)
- Peeled and Sliced Ginger (2 tbls)
- Peeled and Crushed Garlic Cloves (5)
- Quartered Onion (1)
- Toasted Sesame Oil (1 tsp)
- Chopped Green Onions (2 stalks, discard whites)
- Dried Ramen Noodles (6 oz)

What to Do:

- Season pork with salt and pepper to taste then sear on all sides in a pan until golden brown.

- In the slow cooker, add the stock, pork, mushrooms, ginger, garlic, and onions

- Heat on high for about 4 or 5 hours.

- Remove pork when done and cut into desired pieces.

- Strain the broth mixture and discard the solids.

- Put broth back in the slow cooker.

- Set to high.

- Add miso paste and ponzu with whisk.

- Add cut pork. Add noodles and cook 4 to 6 mins.

- Heat peas in a skillet until they become bright green.

- Divide ramen into individual bowls. Top with pork, scallions, peas and other dressings.

Chicken Ramen Recipes

Basic Low Sodium Chicken Ramen

This recipe needs 10 mins to prepare, 20 minutes to cook and will make 4 servings.

What to Use:

- Chopped Chives (2 tbsp)
- Grated Carrot (1)
- Baby Spinach (3 cups)
- Refrigerated Yaki Soba Noodles (3 small packages, noodles only)
- Soy Sauce (1 tbsp)
- Shiitake Mushrooms (4 oz)
- Low Sodium Chicken Broth (4 cups)
- Grated Ginger (1 tbsp)
- Minced Garlic (4 cloves)
- Olive Oil (1 tbsp)
- Large Eggs (2)

What to Do:

- First make the eggs. Fill a large pot with water, enough to fully submerge both eggs. Take the eggs and boil them for 1 min. Then remove the eggs from the heat source and place to the side, covered, for an additional 8-10 mins. When the time has completed, drain the water and let both eggs cool before processing them to be incorporated into the dish.

- Pour oil in a large pot. On medium heat, add grated ginger and minced garlic. Stir this for about 1-2 minutes until aromatic.

- Then, add chicken broth, soy sauce, mushrooms and 3 cups of water. Whisk this combination of ingredients.

- Bring the mixture to a boil then reduce the heat and simmer it for 10 mins. Mushrooms should be soft.

- Add Yaki-Soba noodles and stir for 2-3 mins. (Any flavor pouches that came with the noodles will not be needed.)

- Add spinach, grated carrots and chopped chives. Stir 2 mins.

- Garnish with the finished eggs, now peeled and chopped in half.

- Serve immediately and enjoy.

Chicken Ramen

This recipe takes 5 mins. to prepare, 20 mins. to make and will make 6 servings.

- Protein: 5.1g
- Total Carbohydrate: 27.1g
- Total Fat: 7.5g
- Calories: 189

What to Use:

- Crunchy Panko Crumbs (optional)
- Sriracha
- Shredded Carrots (1 cup)
- Chopped Kale (2 cups)
- Chopped Scallions or Chives (.5 cups)
- Instant Ramen Noodles
- Dried Shiitake Mushrooms (1 oz)
- Water (4 cups)
- Chicken Broth (4 cups)
- Grated Garlic (4 tsps)
- Grated Ginger (3 tsps)
- Sesame Oil (1 tbsp)

What to Do:

- First take a large pot and begin to heat the sesame oil. Medium heat will suffice.

- Then you will add your grated garlic and ginger, which you will stir until aromatic.

- At this point, add 4 cups broth and water. Bring to a boil, then reduce heat to a simmer.

- Add the dried shiitake mushrooms. Stir, then allow to cook, covered, for 10 mins. The mushrooms should be soft.

- To the mixture, add noodles and scallions. Let it simmer for 5 mins.

- Then remove from heat and add carrots and kale.

- Serve immediately and top with Panko Crumbs. (For golden crispy panko crumbs, toss them in oil and toast them in oven until they are golden brown.)

- Enjoy

This recipe takes about 15 mins to make and makes 1 serving.

- Protein: 44.5g
- Total Carbohydrates: 17.4g
- Total Fat: 14.3g
- Calories: 389

What to Use:

- Chicken Broth (1 cup)
- Ramen Noodle Pack Creamy Chicken(1)
- Mixed Veggies (2 cups)
- Chopped Onion (1 cup)
- Oil of Choice (2 tsp)

What to Do:

- Deep fry or bake chicken nuggets, or microwave if already cooked. Set aside.

- Heat oil in a skillet on medium high, then add mixed veggies and onions.

- Add broth and seasonings to pan. Bring to a boil.

- Add noodles. Reduce to simmer and cook for about 2 mins.

- Chop chicken nuggets into pieces.

- Serve ramen. Place chicken nuggets on top.

Spicy Chicken Ramen

This recipe will take 15 mins. prep time, 10 mins. to make, to make and will make 4 servings.

What to Use:

- Toasted Sesame Oil (1 tbls)
- Vegetable Oil (2 tbls)
- Scallions
- Mirin (3 tbls)
- Fresh Ginger (2 inches)
- Garlic (6 cloves)
- Sambal Oelek (3 tbls)
- White Miso (.5 cups)
- Red Miso (.5 cups)
- Chopped Yellow Onion (small)
- Ramen Noodles (6 oz)
- Unsweetened Soy Milk (2 cups)
- Chicken Stock (3 to 4 cups)
- Shiitake Mushrooms (5 oz)
- Eggs (4)
- Oil (1 tbls)
- Extra Firm Tofu (12 to 15 oz)
- Roasted Seaweed
- A food processor and tofu press

What to Do:

- First begin to make the spicy miso paste. This will give the ramen its spicy flavor. Place the yellow onion, red miso, white miso, sambal oelek, garlic, ginger, mirin, oil and sesame oil into the food processor. Process the ingredients until a thick past forms. Place it to the side.

- Using a tofu press, remove moisture from the tofu then cut it into cubes. Then fry the pieces in a large pot with oil until brown.

- Add .25 cups of the spicy miso paste to the pot. Cook for 1 min. then take it out of the pan and place it on a plate.

- Add the chicken broth to the remains left in the pot for flavor.

- Add mushrooms and a Tbls of the spicy miso paste and brown.

- Then add the broth and soy milk. Bring to a boil then reduce to a simmer.

- Take .5 cups of the spicy miso paste and place into a fine strainer and place it halfway into the pot. Stir and allow the past to slowly dissolve into the mixture. Remove the remaining debris inside strainer.

- Season with soy sauce to taste.

- Fill a large pot with water, enough to fully submerge both eggs. Take the eggs and boil them for 1 min. Then remove the eggs from the heat source and place to the side, covered, for an additional 8-10 mins. When the time has completed, drain the water and let both eggs cool before processing them to be incorporated into the dish.

- Follow package instructions to cook noodles separately. Strain then add noodles to individual bowls for serving. Pour the spicy broth onto noodles. Add tofu proportionately.

- Serve immediately. Dress with eggs, scallions and roasted seaweed. Save remaining spicy miso paste or freeze for later use.

Miso Chicken Ramen

This recipe takes 30 mins prep, 30 mins to cook and makes 4 servings.

- Protein: 28g
- Total Carbohydrate: 33g
- Total Fat: 16g
- Calories: 383

What to Use:

- Shiitake Mushrooms (2 cups sliced)
- Broken Chinese Noodles (4 oz)
- Bok Choy (8 cups)
- Boneless Skinless Chicken Thighs Cut into pieces (1.25 lbs)
- Reduced Sodium Soy Sauce (1.5 tbls)
- White Miso (3 tbls)
- Water (4 cups)
- Finely Grated Ginger (1 tbls)
- Minced Garlic Cloves (4)
- Scallions (1 bunch) (separate white and green)
- Toasted Sesame Oil (2 tbls, divided)

What to Do:

- Heat a single tbls of oil in a big pot on medium high heat.

- Add the white scallions, ginger, garlic, and cook until aromatic.

- Add water, soy sauce, miso, and the last tbls of oil. Bring to a boil.

- Add chicken, bok choy and mushrooms.

- Reduce to a simmer and stir occasionally until the chicken is cook and veggies are soft. This should take 3 to 5 mins.

- Serve. Add green scallions on top.

Rotisserie Chicken Ramen

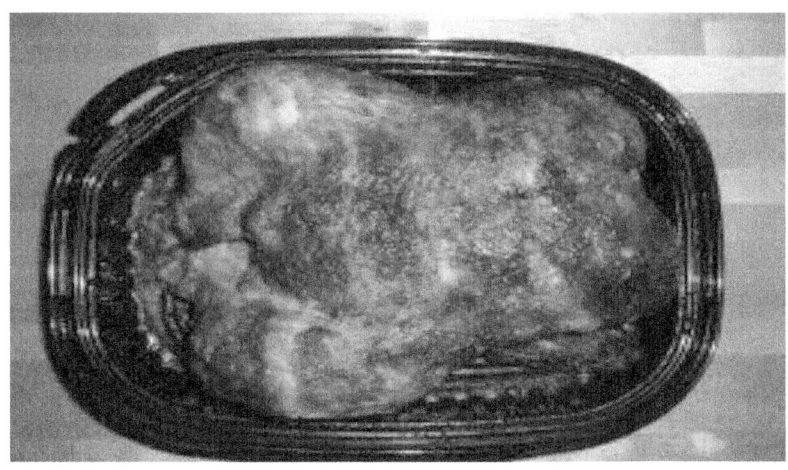

This recipe takes 10 mins. to prep, 25 mins. to cook and makes 6 servings.

- Protein: 32g
- Total Carbohydrate: 72g
- Total Fat: 34g
- Calories: 724

What to Use:

- Scallions (1 bunch)
- Ramen Noodles (20 Oz)
- Beef Broth (2 Cups)
- Eggs (3)
- Mushrooms (2 Cups)
- Chile Garlic Sauce
- Shredded Rotisserie Chicken (3 Cups)
- Soy Sauce (2 Tbls)
- Chicken Broth (4 Cups)
- Salt and Pepper
- Olive Oil (1 Tbls)

What to Do:

- Saute the mushrooms for about 5 mins. with oil and season with salt and pepper. Place it aside.

- Fill a pot with water, enough to fully submerge eggs. Take the eggs and boil them for 1 min. Then remove the eggs from the heat source and place to the side, covered, for an additional 8-10 mins. When the time has completed, drain the water and let both eggs cool before processing them to be incorporated into the dish.

- Combine the chicken and beef broths in a large pot together with soy sauce. Bring to a boil then immediately reduce to a simmer.

- Add ramen and cook for 4 mins.

- Serve immediately. Top each individual bowl with shredded chicken, sliced scallions and garlic sauce.

- Garnish with peeled, halved egg.

Hearty Chicken Breast Ramen

This recipe takes 10 mins prep, 20 mins to cook and makes 4 servings.

- Protein: 31.3g
- Total Carbohydrate: 38g
- Total Fat: 5.8
- Calories: 339

What to Use:

- Hot Chili Oil
- Chopped Green Onions (2)
- Shredded Carrots (1 cup)
- Sliced Cabbage (1 cup)
- Ramen Noodles (6 to 8 oz)
- Chicken Breast Fillets (2)
- Low Sodium Soy Sauce (1.5 tsp)
- Low Sodium Chicken Broth (4 cups)
- Eggs (2)

What to Do:

- Fill a pot with water, enough to fully submerge eggs. Take the eggs and boil them for 1 min. Then remove the eggs from the heat source and place to the side, covered, for an additional 8-10 mins. When the time has completed, drain the water and let both eggs cool before processing them to be incorporated into the dish.

- In a large pot bring your chicken broth and soy sauce to a boil then add the chicken breasts. Cook until done, which should be about 8 to 10 minutes.

- Remove the breasts from the broth and shred the chicken. Return the now shredded chicken to the broth along with ramen noodles.

- Cook for an additional 3 to 5 mins. or as directed by ramen packaging.

- Add seasoning to taste.

- Remove from the stove and add carrots. Add cabbage.

- Serve immediately.

- Garnish each serving with chili oil and chopped onion to taste.

- Garnish with peeled, halved eggs.

Spicy Chicken Ramen Version 2

This recipe takes 30 mins to make and makes 3 servings.

- Protein: 60g
- Total Carbohydrate: 57g
- Total Fat: 27g
- Calories: 710

What to Use:

- Spinach (Palmful)
- Rice Vinegar (1 Tbls)
- Sriracha Sauce (2 Tbls)
- Soy Sauce (2 Tbls)
- Grated Ginger (Thumb-sized)
- Grate Garlic Cloves (2)
- Rotisserie Chicken
- Water (2 Cups)
- Chicken Stock (1 Qrt)
- Ramen Noodles (9 Oz)
- Sliced Thai Chillies
- Sriracha Sauce
- Eggs (2)
- Scallions
- Dried Seaweed

What to Do:

- Fill a pot with water, enough to fully submerge eggs. Take the eggs and boil them for 1 min. Then remove the eggs from the heat source and place to the side, covered, for an additional 8-10 mins. When the time has completed, drain the water and let both eggs cool before processing them to be incorporated into the dish.

- Take all ingredients, except for sriracha, eggs, scallions and seaweed, and boil them in a large pot. Boil then reduce to a simmer.

- Bring water to a boil in a separate pot.Cook ramen until tender, about 3 mins. Then strain.

- Add noodles to individuals bowls and pour broth mix on top.

- Add sriracha, peeled and halved eggs, scallions and seaweed to taste.

Slow Cooker Chicken Ramen

This recipe takes to 10 mins. prep time, 3 hours to make and makes 4 serving. This recipe is more easy than quick, but is an additional set it and forget it option that is very low maintenance if you have time.

- Protein: 33g
- Total Carbohydrate: 33g
- Total Fat: 10g
- Calories: 367

What to Use:
- Ramen Noodles (3 oz)
- Black Pepper (.5 tsp)
- Ground Ginger (.5 tsp)
- Sliced Mushrooms (4 oz)
- Unsweetened Soy Milk (.5 cups)
- Seasoned Rice Vinegar (.25 cups)
- Soy Sauce (.25 cups)
- Chicken Broth (4 cups)
- Minced Garlic Cloves (3)
- Diced Yellow Onion (half)
- Boneless Chicken Breasts
- Toppings: Chopped Cilantro, Sliced Green Onions, Sliced Carrots, Sliced Jalapenos, Crushed Red Peppers, Sesame Seeds, Sesame Oil, Spinach, Eggs (4).

What to Do:

- Fill a pot with water, enough to fully submerge eggs. Take the eggs and boil them for 1 min. Then remove the eggs from the heat source and place to the side, covered, for an additional 8-10 mins. When the time has completed, drain the water and let both eggs cool before processing them to be incorporated into the dish.

- Oil the bottom of your crockpot then place all of the ingredients inside. Do not place toppings inside!

- Cook on low, covered with top, for 3 hrs.

- At the end of the cook time, take cooked chicken from the crockpot and place to the side for cutting/chopping.

- Add ramen noodles and turn heat to high.

- Cook for an additional 5 mins. Covered.

- Add chicken to main mixture or to individual servings, whichever is preferred.

- Serve and add any combination of toppings and seasonings.

Big Bowl Chicken Ramen

This chicken ramen is a larger, yet easy recipe. Prep time is 35 mins, and cook time is 35 mins. This recipe makes 8 servings.

- Protein: 27.66g
- Total Carbohydrate: 59.4g
- Fat: 25.27g
- Calories: 571

What to Use:

- Green Onions
- Fresh Ramen Noodles (1.5 lbs)
- Shredded Chicken (3 cups)
- Button Mushrooms (4 oz)
- Low Sodium Chicken Broth (8 cups)
- Peeled Chopped Ginger (2 inches)
- Chopped Garlic Cloves (4)
- Trimmed and Chopped Leek (1)
- Chopped Yellow Onion (1)
- Canola Oil (3 tbls)
- Sesame Oil
- Soy Sauce
- Large Eggs (8)

What to Do:

- Fill a pot with water, enough to fully submerge eggs. Take the eggs and boil them for 1 min. Then remove the eggs from the heat source and place to the side, covered, for an additional 8-10 mins. When the time has completed, drain the water and let both eggs cool before processing them to be incorporated into the dish.

- In a large pot use 2 Tbls oil and cook onion. Sear until brown, but do not stir.

- Add garlic, ginger and bit of broth. Stir until remains are cleaned from the bottom of the pan. Pour the rest of the broth.

- Bring to medium low heat and cover. Simmer for 30 mins.

- Strain broth with fine mesh strainer into a bowl. Remove remains and set broth mixture to the side.

- Use the same pot to heat another Tbls of oil. Cook mushrooms until tender. Add chicken and broth. Simmer. Add soy sauce and seasonings to taste.

- Cook noodles separately and divide into serving bowls.

- Pour broth over noodles and add toppings and peeled halved eggs.

Chicken Ramen with Brown Sugar

This recipe takes 15 mins total. It requires a food processor and creates about 4 small servings.
- Protein: 8g
- Total Carbohydrate: 37g
- Fat: 9g
- Calories: 260

What to Use:
- Chopped Broccoli (2 cups)
- Diced Green Onions (1 cup)
- Cooked Ramen Noodles (4 cups)
- Brown Sugar (.25 cups)
- Sesame Oil (4 tbls)
- Shichimi Togarashi (1tsp)
- Ginger Root (1 tbls)
- Green Curry Paste (2 tsp)
- Rice Wine Vinegar (.3 cups)
- Soy Sauce (.3 cups)
- Chicken Broth (4 cups)

What to Do:
- Take brown sugar, curry paste, vinegar, soy sauce, broth, shichimi togarashi, ginger and sesame oil and place into processor.

- Process on low then incrementally shift into higher settings until you reach the highest speed. This process should take about 5 mins. so don't rush it.

- Cook noodles

- Heat broth.

- Add together in serving bowls.

- Garnish with green onions and toppings, season to taste.

- Enjoy

Chicken and Veggie Ramen

This recipe take 10 mins. to pre, 8 mins. to cook. This recipe makes 3 servings.

- Protein: 15g
- Total Carbohydrate: 49g
- Fat: 14g
- Calories: 444

What to Use:

- Chopped Cabbage (2 cups)
- Sliced Red Bell Pepper (1)
- Thin Sliced Carrot (1)
- Water (1.25 cups)
- Chopped Chicken Thighs (7 oz)
- Onion (.5)
- Garlic Gloves (2)
- Oil (1 Tbsp)
- Ramen (2 packets)
- Chopped Green Onions
- Mirin (1 tbsp)
- Hoisin Sauce (2 Tsp)
- Oyster Sauce (1 Tbsp)
- Dark Soy Sauce (1 Tbsp)

What to Do:

- Mix soy sauce, oyster sauce, hoisin sauce, and mirin in a bowl.

- Heat skillet, add oil, onions and garlic. Brown for 1 min.

- Add chicken to the pan. Brown chicken pieces.

- Add sauce mixture.

- Cook until caramelized. About 1 min.

- Add capsicum.

- Add carrots.

- Push veggies and chicken to one side of the pan then add the water.

- When the water starts to bubble along the edged, add the ramen to the side of bubbling water.

- After 45 secs. turn the ramen over and cook for an additional 35 seconds.

- Toss noodles, chicken, veggies and sauce together.

- Add cabbage.

- Toss.

- Let the mixture reduce.

- Serve and garnish with green onions and favorite toppings.

Chicken Ramen With Spicy Peanut Sauce

This recipe take 5 mins. Prep, 10 mins. to make and makes 4 servings.

- Protein: 33g
- Total Carbohydrate: 50g
- Fat: 33g
- Calories: 623

What to Use:

- Chopped Peanuts (.5 Cups)
- Shredded Chicken (2 Cups)
- Ramen Noodles (3 Oz)
- Soy Sauce (3 Tbls)
- Creamy Peanut Butter (3 Tbls)
- Sriracha Chili Sauce
- Chopped
- Green Onions (2)

What to Do:

- In a large bowl, mix peanut butter, soy sauce and sriracha. Mix it until the ingredients blend.

- Microwave 30 secs.

- Whisk until peanut butter melts down. Sauce will be a bit thick.

- Get a large pot. Boil 6 cups of water.

- Use 3 packets of seasonings from the ramen packets.

- Add noodles. Cook until tender, until 3 mins. Or as directed.

- Separate noodles and broth.

- Add chicken and sauce to hot noodles.

- Add broth slowly until desired consistency is reached.

- Garnish with peanuts and green onions.

- Enjoy.

Work Week Chicken Ramen

This recipe takes 3 mins to prep, 15 mins to make and creates 1 serving.

- Protein: 38g
- Total Carbohydrate: 9g
- Total Fat: 10g
- Calories: 279

What to Use:

- Chicken Broth or Stock (2 cups)
- Swiss Chard (1 leaf)
- Red Bed Pepper (one-eighth)
- Carrot (small)
- Ramen Packet
- Chicken Breast (100g)
- Egg (1)

What to Do:

- Fill a pot with water, enough to fully submerge egg. Take the egg and boil for 1 min. Then remove the egg from the heat source and place to the side, covered, for an additional 8-10 mins. When the time has completed, drain the water and let the egg cool before processing it to be incorporated into the dish.

- In a frying pan, heat oil and pour in bite size pieces of the chicken breast. (note: don't let the pieces touch as they cook.)

- Your pieces should be small so it should only take a little less than a minute on each side.

- Add your chicken stock to the pan, as well as veggies.

- Let it boil for 1 min.

- Add noodles to your large serving bowl. Pour the broth on top and let sit for 2 mins or until noodles are al dente. Stir and dress with egg.

- Enjoy.

Sesame Chicken Salad Ramen

This recipe takes 10 mins prep, 20 mins to cook and makes 4 servings.

- Protein: 50g
- Total Carbohydrate: 70g
- Total Fat: 39g
- Calories: 828

What to Use:

- Lime (cut into wedges)
- Sriracha (.25 cups)
- Fresno Chiles (2)
- Chopped Cilantro (.25 cups)
- Chopped Green Onion (2, colors separated)
- Eggs (4)
- Ramen Packs (4)
- Boneless, Skinless Chicken Tenders or Thighs
- Kosher Salt (2 tsp)
- Miso Paste (1 tbls)
- Reduced Sodium Soy Sauce (3 tbls)
- Low Sodium Chicken or Vegetable Broth (8 cups)
- Minced Garlic Cloves (2)
- Minced Ginger (1 tbls)
- Sesame Oil (1 tbls)
- Eat Smart Sesame Salad Kit (1 bag)

What to Do:

- Fill a pot with water, enough to fully submerge eggs. Take the eggs and boil them for 1 min. Then remove the eggs from the heat source and place to the side, covered, for an additional 8-10 mins. When the time has completed, drain the water and let both eggs cool before processing them to be incorporated into the dish.

- Over a medium-high heat, cook ginger for about two mins then add garlic and the veggies form the salad kit. Cook for about 4 mins. Cabbage should be well wilted.

- Then, add the miso paste, salt, chicken, soy sauce, and stock to a pot. Bring to a boil then add chicken.

- Reduce to simmer and cook for 5 mins.

- After that, take the chicken from the pot and place on a baking sheet. Brush the chicken with dressing from the salad kit, about half of it.

- Broil chicken for 5 mins.

- Add Ramen Packs to the boiling broth. Add sauteed veggies. Simmer for about 2 mins.

- Divide contents in serving bowls, top with chicken pieces, peeled, halved eggs and your favorite toppings.

Low-Cal Chicken Ramen

This recipe takes 5 mins to prep, 8 mins to cook and makes 1 serving.

- Protein: 5g
- Total Carbohydrates: 7g
- Total Fat: 1g
- Calories: 80

What to Use:

- Pepper (pinch)
- Ginger (pinch)
- Yeast Flakes (.25 tsp)
- Garlic Powder (.25 tsp)
- Garlic Salt (.25 tsp)
- Onion Powder (.5 tsp)
- Salt (1 tbls)
- Low Calorie Chicken Broth (2 cups)
- Shirataki Noodles (1 package)

What to Do:

- Rinse and strain noodles.

- Add salt then continue rinsing.

- Pour chicken broth into a large pot.

- Add noodles and bring the pot to a boil.

- Combine all your other ingredients, seasonings and yeast, into a bowl.

- Add seasonings to the pot when it begins to boil.

- Cook, stirring occasionally, for 3 mins.

Low Carb Keto Chicken Ramen

This recipe takes 15 mins prep, 17 mins cook time and makes 4 servings.

- Protein: 35g
- Total Carbohydrate: 17g
- Total Fat: 14g
- Calories: 290

What to Use:
- Cilantro Leaves
- Scallions (4)
- Miracle Noodles (Shirataki Noodles)
- Eggs (4)
- Rotisserie Chicken
- Salt
- Pepper
- Coconut Aminos or Soy Sauce (2.5 tbls)
- Better than Bouillon (2.5 tbls)
- Water (8 cups)

What to Do:

- Fill a pot with water, enough to fully submerge eggs. Take the eggs and boil them for 1 min. Then remove the eggs from the heat source and place to the side, covered, for an additional 8-10 mins. When the time has completed, drain the water and let both eggs cool before processing them to be incorporated into the dish.

- Bring all the water (8 cups) to a boil.

- Add bouillon, coconut or soy sauce to the pan.

- Add pieces of rotisserie chicken to your liking.

- Rinse and strain shirataki noodles.

- Add noodles to the broth, boil for time determined on packaging.

- Garnish with cilantro leaves, and peeled, halved eggs.

- Enjoy

Ramen Noodles with Canned Chicken

This recipe takes 37 mins and makes 4 servings.

- Protein: 24g
- Total Carbohydrates: 57g
- Total Fat: 13g
- Calories: 480

What to Use:

- Spring Onion (2 stalks)
- Corn (150 g)
- Shiitake Mushrooms (200 g)
- Ramen Noodles (250 g)
- Bok Choy (2 stalks)
- Sesame Oil (.5 tsp)
- Soy Sauce (dribble)
- Ginger (2 inches)
- Lemongrass (1 stalk)
- Onion (1)
- Garlic Cloves (4)
- Vegetable Stock (2 liters)
- Canned Chicken (2)

What to Do:

- Cut mushrooms into slices (without the stems), as well as, spring onion and bok choy.

- Cut garlic cloves and the onion in half, peel ginger, and crush the lemongrass.

- Add veggie stock to a large pot. Bring to a boil and add your cut ingredients.
- Simmer broth for about 30 mins.

- Cook noodles separately as instructed.

- Cook until bok choy is soft and then serve in a bowl with corn toppings and your favorite hot sauce.

- Open tin of chicken. Drain. Then top ramen with chicken to taste.

Beef Ramen Recipes

Ramen Noodles with Mongolian Beef

This recipes takes 20 mins. to prep, 30 mins. to make and creates 4 servings.

- Protein: 46g
- Total Carbohydrate: 75g
- Total Fat: 42g
- Calories: 870

What to Use:

- Red Pepper Flakes (.25 Tsp)
- Minced Garlic Cloves (4)
- Chicken Broth (1.25 Cups)
- Brown Sugar (Two Thirds Cups)
- Low Sodium Soy Sauce (Three-Fourths Cup)
- Sesame Oil (2 Tbls)
- Chopped Green Onions (3)
- Ramen Noodles (8 Oz)
- Thin Sliced Green Bell Pepper (1)
- Vegetable Oil (.25 Cups)
- Flank Steak (.5 lbs)

What to Do:

- Cut steak into thin pieces then place in a bag with the corn starch. Cover steak completely.

- Add beef slowly to hot oiled skillet. Add more beef incrementally. Add more oil as needed.

- Remove steak when cooked to appropriate wellness.

- Add bell pepper, soften, then remove from skillet.

- Add chicken broth, sesame oil, garlic, brown sugar, soy sauce, and red pepper flakes.

- Cook for 10 mins. on medium heat.

- Make ramen according to packaging.

- Strain ramen, add noodles, beef and bell peppers to sauce.

- Stir and mix.

- Garnish with green onions and serve immediately.

Ramen with Beef and Broccoli

This recipe takes 15 minutes to prep, 10 mins to cook, has options to marinate steak, and makes 4 servings.

- Protein: 29g
- Total Carbohydrate: 18g
- Total Fat: 29g
- Calories: 360

What to Use:
- Sesame Seeds
- Sriracha (.5 Tsp)
- Brown Sugar (1 Tbls)
- Rice Wine Vinegar (2 Tbls)
- Low Sodium Soy Sauce (6 Tbls)
- Oyster Sauce (6 Tbls)
- Cornstarch (2 Tbls)
- Sesame Oil (2 Tsp)
- Ginger (1 Tbls)
- Low Sodium Beef Broth (Three-Fourths Cup)
- Water (.25 Cups)
- Ramen Noodle (3 Packets)

What to Do:

- (Optional) In a medium to large bowl, add a tbls of soy sauce and rice wine. Marinate steak in the refrigerator for 1 hour or longer for up to a day for deeper flavor. Mix water, beef broth, ginger, sesame oil, cornstarch, oyster sauce, soy sauce and rice wine vinegar, as well as brown sugar and sriracha to taste into a bowl. Cook Ramen according to packaging. Once done, drain and remove. Saute broccoli with oil until crisp. Set broccoli aside. Remaining tbls of oil should be put back into the pan and heated until it nearly reaches its smoking point. Add beef and saute for about 1 or 2 mins. Then add garlic until aromatic. Then broccoli. Then noodles. Stir and serve immediately. Garnish with sesame seeds and favorite toppings.

Low-Cal Beef Ramen

This recipe takes 5 mins to prep, 8 mins to cook and makes 1 serving.

- Protein: 5g
- Total Carbohydrates: 7g
- Total Fat: 1g
- Calories: 80

What to Use:

- Pepper (pinch)
- Ginger (pinch)
- Yeast Flakes (.25 tsp)
- Garlic Powder (.25 tsp)
- Garlic Salt (.25 tsp)
- Onion Powder (.5 tsp)
- Salt (1 tbls)
- Low Calorie Beef Broth (2 cups)
- Shirataki Noodles (1 package)

What to Do:

- Rinse and strain noodles.

- Add salt then continue rinsing.

- Pour beef broth into a large pot.

- Add noodles and bring the pot to a boil.

- Combine all your other ingredients, seasonings and yeast, into a bowl.

- Add seasonings to the pot when it begins to boil.

- Cook, stirring occasionally, for 3 mins.

Spicy Beef Ramen Soup

This recipe takes 7 mins. prep, 20 minutes to cook, and makes 4 servings.

- Protein: 10g
- Total Carbohydrate: 8g
- Total Fat: 23g
- Calories: 200

What to Use:
- Baby Spinach
- Beef Strips
- Parsley (2 Tbls)
- Chopped Green Onions (.25 Cups)
- Eggs (2)
- Sriracha Sauce (1 Tbls)
- Water (4 Cups)
- Vegetable Stock (1.5 Cups)
- Chopped Ginger (1 Tsp)
- Chopped Garlic Cloves (1)
- Peeled and Cut Carrots (2)
- Pepper (.25 Tsp)
- Salt (.25 Tsp)
- Olive Oil (2 Tbls)
- Ramen Noodle Packs (2)

What to Do:
- In a skillet heat oil on medium heat. Add carrots, ginger, garlic and onions.Cook for about 5 mins.

- Combine with water and broth. Bring to a boil until veggies are soft. Then add Ramen and cook for an additional 5 to 10 mins. Or until tender.

- Cook beef in a different skillet until appropriate wellness.

- Add to noodle dish.

- Serve and enjoy with toppings.

Ground Beef Ramen Skillet

This recipe takes 25 mins altogether to prepare and makes 4 servings.

- Protein: 49g
- Total Carbohydrate: 18g
- Total Fat: 9g
- Calories: 160

What to Use:

- Beef Flavored Ramen Packs (6 Oz)
- Ground Ginger (1 Tsp)
- Soy Sauce (3 Tbls)
- Beef Broth (2 Cups)
- Stir Fry Veggies (12 Oz)

What to Do:

- Using 1 Tbls of oil, brown the beef then drain the excess liquid.

- Continue cooking on medium high heat and add stir fry veggies and cook for 2 to 3 mins.

- Combine soy sauce, broth, ginger, and a packet of seasoning mix into a bowl.

- Mix until well blended then pour the mixture into the skillet.

- Reduce the heat to a simmer and stir.

- Cook for about 5. mins or until done.

- Serve immediately

Oriental Beef Ramen Noodles

This recipe takes 35 mins. to prepare, makes 4 servings,

- Protein: 31g
- Total Carbohydrate: 31g
- Total Fat: 4g
- Calories: 360

What to Use:

- Grated Ginger (1 Tbls)
- Minced Garlic (2 Tbls)
- Chopped Onion (.5 Cups)
- Water (4 Cups)
- Vegetable Oil (2 Tsp)
- Oriental Ramen Packet (2)
- Pepper (1 Tsp)
- Top Beef Sirloin Steak Boneless (1 lb)
- Toppings: Bamboo Shoots, Baby Spinach, Sliced Green Onions, Mushrooms, Sugar Snap peas, Shredded Carrots, Bean Sprouts.

What to Do:

- Slice steak in strips.

- Add oil and beef to a pan with .5 ramen packet seasoning and pepper.

- Stir fry for 1 to 2 mins. If you need to, season beef first and fry in two batches.
- Place cooked beef to the side.

- Add the onion, garlic, ginger, the remaining .5 of seasoning in the packet and water to the same skillet used for the beef. Bring to a boil then reduce to a simmer.

- Simmer 2 mins.

- Add noodles and bring to a boil again, then add noodles and cook for about 3 mins.

- Add beef and miso.

- Serve immediately.

Ramen Mason Jars

This recipe takes 15 mins. to make and creates 4 servings.

- Protein: 32g
- Total Carbohydrate: 31g
- Total Fat: 6g
- Calories: 400

What to Use:
- Ramen Packets (2 packs)
- Sliced Green Onions (.5 Cup)
- Thin Sliced Mushrooms (8)
- Shredded Carrot (1 Cup)
- Baby Spinach (2 Cups)
- Sesame Oil (8 Drops)
- Red Miso Paste(4 Tsp)
- Kimchi (.5 Cups)
- Beef Base (2 Tbls)
- Thin Sliced Flank Steak (12 Oz)

What to Do:
- In 4 mason canning jars, add 1.5 Tsp of beef concentrate, 1 Tsp miso paste, 2 Tbls kimchi, and 2 drops of the sesame oil.

- Cook steak separately to desired wellness.

- Add .5 cups to each jar.

- Divy up the rest of the ingredients proportionately.

- Add .5 of each packet or ramen to each of the jars.

- Let sit in the fridge for about an hour if beef is hot. Can be refrigerated for up to 3 days before serving.

- When serving, add 1.5 cups of boiling water to each jar, then close and shake. Let it stand for 5 mins.

- Add toppings if desired.

Crock Pot Beef Ramen

This is an 8 hour <u>slow cooker</u> recipe with 20 mins. prep but it is very easy and creates 6 servings.

- Protein: 92g
- Total Carbohydrate: 4g
- Total Fat: 52g
- Calories: 550

What to Use:

- Jalapenos
- Lime Wedges
- Cilantro
- Sliced Green Onions
- Chuka Soba Noodles (1 pack)
- Sliced Mushrooms (2 Cups)
- Brown Sugar (.25 Cups)
- Lime (1)
- Chili Garlic Paste (1 Tbls)
- Ginger (1 Tbls)
- Rice Wine Vinegar (.25 Cups)
- Low Sodium Soy Sauce (.25 Cups)
- Low Sodium Beef Broth (32 Oz. + at least.25 Cups extra)

What to Do:

- Put the brown sugar, lime juice, chili garlic paste, ginger, rice wine vinegar, soy sauce, 32 Oz of beef broth and chuck roast into the slow cooker on low and let it cook covered for 8 hrs.

- After that, shred beef and return to crockpot.

- Set it to high then add mushrooms and cook for an additional 10 mins, covered.

- Then add noodles and continue to cook for 5 more minutes and add the last bit of broth.

- Add to individual bowl and add garnishes.

- Enjoy.

Spicy Beef Ramen Chashu

This recipe takes 105 minutes and makes 4 servings.

- Protein: 35g
- Total Carbohydrate: 31g
- Total Fat: 27g
- Calories: 490

What to Use:

- Chopped Red Chilli Pepper
- Chopped Green Onion
- Eggs (4)
- Enoki Mushroom (1 Pkg)
- Cooking Oil (.25 Cups)
- Chilli Flakes (4 Tbls)
- Black Pepper
- Salt
- Water (8 Cups)
- Cooking Oil (1 Tbs)
- Beef Stock (1 Tbls)
- Sugar (1 Tbls)
- Chopped Green Onion
- Red Chilli Peppers (5)
- Thin Sliced Ginger (3 Cm)
- Shallots (4)
- Garlic Cloves (5)
- Soy Sauce (.25 Cups)
- Ramen Noodles (4 Fresh Packs)
- Beef Shank (400 g)

What to Do:

- Heat the cooking oil to it's smoking point then remove from heat and add chilli flakes.

- Sear the shank in a pressure cooker using oil to grease the bottom. Cook til properly browned on every side.

- Add soy sauce, 6 cups of water, ginger, shallot, garlic, chilli pepper, beef stock powder, green onion, black pepper, and sugar. Boil. Cook for 45 to 60 mins.

- Remove beef and slice thinly.

- Boil mushrooms and noodles.

- Add sugar if the crock pot broth needs it. Add all ingredients to crock pot.

- Serve immediately.

- Garnish with egg and favorite toppings.

Easy Weekday Ramen

This recipe takes 10 mins. prep, 11 mins. to cook and makes 2 to 3 servings.

- Protein: 25g
- Total Carbohydrate: 43g
- Total Fat: 14g
- Calories: 400

What to Use:
- Trimmed Snow Peas (2 Cups)
- Dark Sesame Seed Oil (1 Tsp)
- Hot Chilli- Garlic Sauce (2 Tsp)
- Soy Sauce (2 Tbls)
- Water (.5 Cups)
- Beef (250 to 375g)
- Red Onion
- Beef Ramen Packet (2)

What to Do:
- Bring 4 cups of water to a boil.

- Put noodles in a bowl and pour the boiling water on top of the noodles and let it soak for about 3 minutes.

- Cut beef into thin slices and fry with oil in a frying pan with sliced onion. When the onion gets softer, add 1 packet of seasoning. Add an additional .5 cups water, chilli garlic sauce, soy and sesame oil.

- Stirring often, cook for about 4 mins.

- Add snow peas and cook 2 to 4 mins.

- Serve immediately and enjoy.

Ramen Veggie Skillet

This recipe takes about 15 mins to make and makes 1 serving.

- Protein: 42g
- Total Carbohydrates: 15g
- Total Fat: 11g
- Calories: 340

What to Use:

- Beef Broth (1 cup)
- Beef Ramen Noodle Pack (1)
- Mixed Veggies (2 cups)
- Chopped Onion (1 cup)
- Oil of Choice (2 tsp)
- Heat and Serve Beef Fajita Meat

What to Do:

- Heat oil in a skillet on medium high, then meat until browned.

- Then add mixed veggies and onions.

- Add broth and seasonings. Bring to a boil.

- Add noodles. Reduce to simmer and cook for about 2 mins.

- Serve

Beef and Garlic Ramen

This recipe takes 25 mins. to prep, 10 mins to cook and makes 4 to 6 servings.

- Protein: 22.5g
- Total Carbohydrate: 39.6g
- Total Fat: 20.7g
- Calories: 434

What to Use:

- Red Pepper Flakes (1 Tsp)
- Brown Sugar (.5 Cups)
- Minced Ginger (1 Tbls)
- Low Sodium Beef Broth (1 Cup)
- Sesame Oil (2 Tbls)
- Ramen Noodles (2 Packs)
- Assorted Vegetables (8 Oz)
- Vegetable Oil (3 to 5 Tbls)
- Minced Garlic (1.5 Tbls)
- Hoisin Sauce (2 Tbls)
- Low Sodium Soy Sauce
- Flank Steak (1 lb)

What to Do:

- Heat a Tbls of oil. Add mixed veggies. Cook until tender.

- Remove veggies and place to the side. Remove skillet from heat.
- Coat beef with cornstarch in a plastic bag.

- Add more oil and heat until smoke point.

- Add beef, sear on each side. Remove and place to the side.

- Now pour the .5 cup and tbls of soy sauce, sesame oil, beef stock, 1.5 tbls of minced garlic, ginger, red pepper flakes and brown sugar. Stir. Cook for about 10 to 12 mins.

- Whisk in a small bowl the remaining cornstarch and 1 Tsp of water, then add to ramen mix.

- Prepare noodles as instructed on packaging. Drain. Rinse in cold water.

- Combine all ingredients and add pepper to taste.

- Serve immediately.

Keto Beef Ramen Bowl

This recipe takes 15 mins. total so it's super simple and makes 2 servings.

- Protein: 39g
- Total Carbohydrate: 8g
- Total Fat: 12g
- Calories: 300

What to Use:

- Minced Ginger (.25 Tsp)
- Minced Garlic Clove (1)
- Apple Cider Vinegar (1 Tbsp)
- Low Sodium Soy Sauce (1 Tbsp)
- Beef Broth (4 Cups)
- Sriracha
- Sliced Beef (.5 lbs)
- Egg (1)
- Bean Sprouts (1 Cup)
- Spiralized Zucchini (2)
- Grape Seed Oil (1 Tsp)

What to Do:

- First make the eggs. Fill a large pot with water, enough to fully submerge both eggs. Take the eggs and boil them for 1 min. Then remove the eggs from the heat source and place to the side, covered, for an additional 8-10 mins. When the time has completed, drain the water and let both eggs cool before processing them to be incorporated into the dish

- Bring broth, soy sauce, vinegar, garlic, and ginger to a boil in a large pot.

- Grease a skillet with grapeseed oil and sear beef slices on both sides. Remove and slice to desired pieces.

- Put the zucchini noodles and scallions and bean sprouts in the broth for 2 minutes.

- Serve in two individual bowls and top with beef on top. Dress with peeled, halved egg.

- Garnish with Sriracha if desired.

Spicy Keto Beef Ramen

This recipe takes 15 mins. to prep, 15 mins. to make and makes 2 servings.

- Protein: 49g
- Total Carbohydrate: 9g
- Total Fat: 77g
- Calories: 937

What to Use:

- Cilantro (4 Tbls)
- Chili Flakes (.5 Tsp)
- Sesame Seeds (1 Tbls)
- Salt
- Pepper
- Sesame Oil (3 Tbls)
- Shirataki Noodles (7 Oz)
- Bok Choy (10 Oz)
- Scallions (2 Oz)
- Water (2 Cups)
- Meat Bouillon Cubes (2)
- Coconut Oil (3 Tbsp)
- Eggs (4)
- Ribeye Steaks (.75 lb)
- Sriracha Sauce (1 Tbsp)
- Minced Garlic Cloves (2)

What to Do:

- First make the eggs. Fill a large pot with water, enough to fully submerge both eggs. Take the eggs and boil them for 1 min. Then remove the eggs from the heat source and place to the side, covered, for an additional 8-10 mins. When the time has completed, drain the water and let both eggs cool before processing them to be incorporated into the dish.

- In a big bowl, mix the garlic and sriracha sauce.

- Slice beef into thin strips then place them into the sriracha mix and let it sit for 10 minutes.

- Once the time is up, heat coconut oil in a skillet and cook beef strips for a few mins. Stir occasionally and cook evenly, adding salt and pepper to taste.

- Rinse ramen noodles with cold water.

- Prepare the broth by adding bouillon cubes and water to a boil. Lower to a simmer and add noodles, which will cool for 2 to 3 mins or as directed.

- Remove the pot from the heat source.

- Put the veggies and beef into individual bowls and top with broth and toppings.

- Serve immediately.

Ramen with Bison

This recipe uses bison, which is a good substitute for beef. This recipe takes 10 mins to prep, 30 mins to prepare and makes 4 servings.

- Protein: 53g
- Total Carbohydrate: 71g
- Total Fat: 18g
- Calories: 640

What to Use:
- Water Chestnuts (drained, chopped) 1 can
- Parsley (2 tbls)
- Fine Chopped Romaine Lettuce (2 heads)
- Ramen Noodles Crushed (3 packs)
- Salt
- Pepper
- Beef Broth (6 cups)
- Thai Curry Paste (1 tbls)
- Ground Bison (1.5 lbs)
- Chopped Celery Stalks (4)
- Fine Chopped Kale Leaves (2 cups)
- Chopped Leeks (2)
- Olive Oil (1 tbls)

What to Do:

- In a large pot, heat olive oil.
- On medium heat stir fry leeks, celery, and kale for about 3 mins.
- Add the broth, bison and the curry paste. Add salt and pepper then bring to a boil. Cover and cook for 20 mins.

- Then, add noodles to the broth and cook for 3 to 5 more mins.

- Garnish with chestnuts, parsley and our favorite toppings.

Seafood Ramen Recipes

Crockpot Seafood Ramen

This recipe takes 5 mins to prep and 2 hrs to cook making 4 servings. Use a seafood mix of your choice.

- Protein: 29.5g
- Total Carbohydrate: 27g
- Total Fat: 2.7g
- Calories: 250

What to Use:

- Red Pepper Flakes (pinch)
- Pepper (large pinch)
- Salt (1 tsp)
- Sesame Oil (drizzle)
- Sliced Tomatoes (.5 lbs)
- Chopped Kale (.25 cups)
- Minced Garlic Cloves (2)
- Rice Vinegar (2 tbls)

- Low Sodium Soy Sauce (2 tbls)
- Sliced Green Onions (2)
- Seafood Mix (1 lb)
- Ramen (4 to 6 oz)
- Seafood Broth (64 oz)

What to Do:

- Place all the ingredients in the cooker, but do not include the seafood, kale, or ramen until later.

- Stir often and allow all the ingredients to mix.

- If cooking on a high temperature expect a waiting time between 2 to 3 hours.

- A lower temperature will take a little longer, between 4 to 6 hours.

- After the ingredients have cooked for the expected time include the seafood, kale and ramen and continue cooking for an extra 15 to 30 minutes.

Ramen with Chicken and Shrimp

This recipe takes 20 mins to prep, 15 mins to cook and makes 3 servings.

- Protein: 37.5g
- Total Carbohydrate: 57.7g
- Total Fat: 9g
- Calories: 460

What to Use:

- Chopped Spring Onions (2)
- Sesame Seeds (1 tbls)
- Soy Sauce (2 tbls)
- Minced Red Chile Pepper (1)
- Sliced Imitation Seafood Sticks(3 oz)
- Hot Water (1 cup)
- Miso Paste (2 tbls)
- Rice Vermicelli (1.5 cups)
- Dashi Powder (1 tsp)
- Cold Water (1 pint)
- Shrimp (3.5 oz)
- Chicken Breast Strips (1 breast worth)
- Vegetable Oil (2 tsp)
- Dried Seaweed (1 tbls)

What to Do:

- To begin, add the wakame in a large bowl of cold water, then place aside.

- While the wakame is soaking grab a skillet and over a medium temperature heat cooking oil.

- When heated, add chicken and shrimp and cook for 5 to 10 minutes, or until there is no sign of pink in the center of the chicken and the shrimp has a color
that is a bright pink.

- Next, boil 1 pint of cold water and mix in dashi power, lower the heat to a medium and add vermicelli.

- Blend miso paste and 2 tablespoons of hot dashi broth in a small bowl then add it to the broth, mix well together until the miso has blended together with the other ingredients.

- Lower the heat on the liquid and let it stay at a simmer. In about 2 minutes the noodles should be tender.

- Now take the soaked wakame, drain and add to the broth. Include the seafood sticks, chicken-shrimp mixture, red chile pepper, sesame seeds, soy sauce and stir well.

- If the broth taste is too hot, adding 1 cup of hot water should take some of the fire from the broth.

- Pour the mixture in serving bowls, add a little spring onions and enjoy.

Creamy Tuna Ramen Noodles

This recipe takes 6 mins prep, 5 mins to cook and makes 2 servings.

- Protein: 50g
- Total Carbohydrates: 54g
- Total Fat: 40g
- Calories: 787

What to Use:

- Ramen Packet (1)
- Water (2 cups)
- Butter (2 tbls)
- Reduced Fat Milk (.25 cups)
- Green Onions.
- Small Can of Light Tuna
- Salt
- Pepper

What to Do:

- Boil water.

- Add noodles and cook for 3 mins.

- Drain the water.

- Open can of Tuna. Drain water.

- Add butter, milk, and seasoning to pot. Stir. Return noodles to pot as well.

- Cook and stir until butter is melting and ingredients have blended.

- Noodles should be coated with a creamy sauce.

- Add tuna, salt and pepper to taste.

- Top with sliced green onions.

Simple Shrimp Ramen

This recipe takes 10 mins to prep, 10 mins to cook and creates 4 servings.

- Protein: 29g
- Total Carbohydrate: 7g
- Total Fat: 7g
- Calories: 219

What to Use:

- Chopped Green Onions
- Cilantro
- Large Shrimp (1lb)
- Ramen Packages (2)
- Sesame Oil (1 tsp)
- Soy Sauce (1 tsp)
- Grated Ginger (1 tbls)
- Seafood Stock (4 cups)
- Minced Garlic Cloves (4)
- Grated Carrot (1)
- Sliced Mushrooms (8 oz)
- Olive Oil (1 to 2 tbls)

What to Do:

- Start by heating olive oil in a large pot, add mushrooms and carrot and saute for 5 minutes or until they start to become tender.

- Next add garlic, and cook for 30 second stirring often.

- After include ginger, broth, soy sauce, and sesame oil, cover and let it cook until the mixture begins to boil.

- As it boils begin adding noodles and shrimp. Again cover and boil for 3 minutes. Once done top it off with chopped green onions and if you should wish add cilantro for that extra special taste.

Low-Cal Seafood Ramen

This recipe takes 5 mins to prep, 8 mins to cook and makes 1 serving.

- Protein: 5g
- Total Carbohydrates: 7g
- Total Fat: 1g
- Calories: 80

What to Use:
- Pepper (pinch)
- Ginger (pinch)
- Yeast Flakes (.25 tsp)
- Garlic Powder (.25 tsp)
- Garlic Salt (.25 tsp)
- Onion Powder (.5 tsp)
- Salt (1 tbls)
- Low Calorie Seafood Stock (2 cups)
- Shirataki Noodles (1 package)

What to Do:
- Rinse and strain noodles.

- Add salt then continue rinsing.

- Pour seafood stock into a large pot.

- Add noodles and bring the pot to a boil.

- Combine all your other ingredients, seasonings and yeast, into a bowl.

- Add seasonings to the pot when it begins to boil.

- Cook, stirring occasionally, for 3 mins.

Shrimp Pho Ramen Soup

This recipe takes 10 mins to prep, 30 mins to cook and makes 4 servings.

- Protein: 31.9g
- Total Carbohydrate: 65g
- Total Fat: 6.3g
- Calories: 450

What to Use:

- Raw Shrimp (1 lb)
- Bok Choy (8 cups)
- Cinnamon (1 tsp)
- Hoisin Sauce (2 tbls)
- Lime Juice (2 tbls)
- Fish Sauce (2 tbls)
- Low Sodium Soy Sauce (2 tbls)
- Lemon Peel (2 strips)
- Chicken Broth (8 cups)
- Chili Garlic Paste (.5 tbls)
- Minced Ginger Root (2 tbls)
- Sesame Oil (1 tbls)
- Black Peppercorns (.5 tsp)
- Cloves (2)
- Coriander Seeds (1 tsp)
- Rice Noodles (8 oz)

What to Do:

- To start, according to package directions prepare rice noodles and place aside.

- Now in a dry pan toast peppercorns, cloves, and coriander over a medium heat and cook for 3 to 5 minutes.

- After, remove from heat and dash mixture with mortar and pestle or spice grinder then set aside.

- Next use a large soup pot and warm sesame oil over medium heat for 30 to 60 seconds, as it start to shimmer add ginger and chili garlic paste and continue to stir for 30 seconds.

- Now add in chicken broth, lemon peel, lime juice, soy sauce, fish sauce, hoisin, cinnamon and toasted spices.

- Allow the mixture to come to a boil then add shrimp and bok choy. As the ingredients continue to simmer cook until the shrimp turns bright pink and the bok choy wilts.

- As a reminder, now would be a good time to check for seasoning and if needed add salt, peper, or soy.

- Finally add rice noodles to four large bowls and pour soup into each. For additional flavor you can add different topping of your choice.

Shrimp Ramen Stir Fry

This recipe take 10 mins to prep, 15 mins to cook and makes 8 servings.

- Protein: 25g
- Total Carbohydrate: 5g
- Total Fat: 13g
- Calories: 259

What to Use:

- Egg
- Low Carb Noodle Packs (14 oz each)
- Broccoli Florets (4 cups)
- Chopped Onion (1 cup)
- Extra Virgin Olive Oil (2 tbls)
- Rice Vinegar (2 tbls)
- Soy Sauce (.25 cups)
- Butter (2 bls)
- Minced Garlic (2 cloves)
- Sesame Oil (2 tbls)
- Shrimp (2 lbs)

What to Do:

- Begin by heating a skillet. Use medium heat to avoid burning.

- Once skillet is heated add sesame oil, ghee, soy sauce, and garlic.

- Return to high heat for boiling.

- Next, add shrimp and be sure to cook them thoroughly. You will not want to see any pink. Let the shrimp stand and move to prepare other ingredients.

- Using the same skillet add more oil,broccoli and onions and use medium heat to cook.Cook broccoli for about 10 minutes. Be sure to cook covered.

- Finally,add noodles to the other ingredients along with the beaten egg and shrimp. Continue to cook on warm.

- Be sure the egg is cooked. Top with parsley, soy sauce and scallions.

Kimchi Seafood Ramen

This recipe takes 5 mins to prep, 25 mins to cook and makes 2 servings.

- Protein: 9g
- Total Carbohydrate: 68g
- Total Fat: 16g
- Calories: 461

What to Use:
- Ramen Pack (150 g)
- Kimchi (.5 cups)
- Salt
- Pepper
- Veggie Broth (6 cups)
- Sesame Oil (.5 tsp)
- Honey (1 tbls)
- Soy Sauce (1.5 tbls)
- Red Chili Flakes (.5 tsp)
- Rice Vinegar (1 tbls)
- Minced Garlic Cloves
- Minced Ginger (1 tbls)
- Olive Oil (2 tsp)
- Favorite Toppings

What to Do:

- Begin this dish by heating olive oil in an appropriate sauce pan. Once the oil is hot enough add so that the oil and ingredients don't stick.

- Add ginger and garlic and saute for 1 minute. It is important to stir constantly. Once heated begin to add the rice vinegar, red chili flakes (Korean).

- For the flavor add soy sauce, sesame oil honey and of course water to thepot continuing to stir well.

- Once ingredient reaches boiling, reduce heat and add seasoning specific for your taste.

- You will not, however need the seasoning from the Ramen noodle packs. You may discard these flavor packets. Once the Ramen noodles have been added continue to cook.

- Once noodles are at desired consistency remove from heat and garnish. Possible garnish suggestions include bean sprouts, extra kimchi, sesame seeds, green onion, hard boiled eggs.

Shrimp and Broccoli Ramen

This recipe takes 10 mins to prep, 20 mins to cook and makes 4 servings.

- Protein: 29g
- Total Carbohydrate: 35g
- Total Fat: 25g
- Calories: 484

What to Use:
- Chopped Parsley
- Vegetable Broth (2 cups)
- Ramen Packs (2)
- Salt
- Pepper
- Broccoli Florets (2 cups)
- Large Onion (1)
- Extra Virgin Olive Oil (4 tbls)
- Butter (1 tbls)
- Shrimp (1 lb)
- Minced Garlic Cloves

What to Do:
- Begin with a large skillet, preferably non-stick.

- Add garlic to the olive oil and cook for only 1 minute, or until the great smell fills the house. Add shrimp and season to your taste. A little salt and pepper should do the trick. Add butter and increase heat to medium high. As butter melts shrimp is pink and brown around the edges.

- Place cooked items on a plate, but do not clean the skillet.Using the same skillet add 2 additional tablespoons of olive oil and broccoli.

- Add noodles and vegetable broth to the skillet and add the shrimp. Return mixture to a boil and cook until noodles are tender. Remove from heat add garnish and parsley. Serve hot.

Seafood Ramen Mix

This recipe takes 15 mins to make and makes 4 servings.

- Protein: 12g
- Total Carbohydrate: 17g
- Total Fat: 4g
- Calories: 148

What to Use:

- Soy Sauce (2 tbls)
- Julienned Carrot (1)
- Chopped Green Onions (.5 cups)
- Seafood Mix (1 cup)
- Oriental Ramen Noodle Pack
- Water (3.5 cups)

What to Do:

- Heat water in a large saucepan, bring to a boil and add the ramen noodles.

- Stir and cook the noodles for about 3 minutes, but do not add seasoning packets.

- Next, add shrimp.carrots. Onion soy sauce and now add the seasoning packets and cook for another 3-4 minutes. Do not overcook.

This recipe takes 10 mins to prep, 20 mins to cook and makes 2 servings.

- Protein: 50g
- Total Carbohydrate: 79.4g
- Total Fat: 80.2g
- Calories: 600

What to Use:

- Garlic Chili Paste (to taste)
- Toasted Sesame Oil (1 tbls)
- Sugar (2 tsp)
- Soy Sauce (2 tbls)
- Shitaake Mushrooms (4 oz)
- Salmon (4 to 6 oz)
- Fresh Ramen Noodles (4 oz)
- Scallions (white part) (3)
- Baby Bok Choy (2)
- Hondashi Granules (.5 tsp)
- Miso Paste (2 tbls)
- Chicken Broth (4 cups)

What to Do:

- To begin this recipe the oven should be set to broil 400F.

- Prepare the marinade for the salmon and shiitakes first.

- To make the marinade stir soy sauce, honey, sesame oil and chili paste together in a small bowl. Once prepared brush the marinade on the salmon and shiitakes.

- Once the marinade is applied broil salmon to your taste.

- Once salmon is cooked, you may begin cooking the noodles and make the broth, allow to simmer. Simmer for a few minutes and add miso, hondashi and stir well. Add the bok choy and scallions, along with wilt. Reduce to a low simmer. Separate noodles into 2 bowls and top with salmon. Garnish is optional and includes:fresh scallions and soft boiled eggs.

Crab and Veggie Ramen

This recipe takes 5 mins to prep, 10 mins to cook and makes 1 serving.

- Protein: 42g
- Total Carbohydrates: 15g
- Total Fat: 11g
- Calories: 340

What to Use:
- Seafood Broth (1 cup)
- Ramen Noodle Pack (1)
- Mixed Veggies (2 cups)
- Chopped Onion (1 cup)
- Oil of Choice (2 tsp)
- Old Bay Seasoning
- Pepper
- Artificial Crab or Cooked Crab

What to Do:

- Heat oil in a skillet on medium high, then add mixed veggies, crab, and onions.

- Add broth and seasoning. Bring to a boil.

- Add noodles. Reduce to simmer and cook for about 2 mins.

- Serve

Salmon and Veggie Ramen Noodles

This recipe takes 35 mins and makes 4 servings

- Protein: 60g
- Total Carbohydrates: 57g
- Total Fat: 24g
- Calories: 572

What to Use:

- Spring Onion (2 stalks)
- Corn (150 g)
- Shiitake Mushrooms (200 g)
- Ramen Noodles (250 g)
- Bok Choy (2 stalks)
- Sesame Oil (.5 tsp)
- Soy Sauce (dribble)
- Ginger (2 inches)
- Lemongrass (1 stalk)
- Onion (1)
- Garlic Cloves (4)
- Vegetable Stock (2 liters)
- Canned Salmon (4)

What to Do:

- Cut mushrooms into slices (without the stems), as well as, spring onion and bok choy.

- Cut garlic cloves and the onion in half, peel ginger, and crush the lemongrass.

- Add veggie stock to a large pot. Bring to a boil and add your cut ingredients.

- Simmer broth for about 30 mins.

- While broth simmers, open tins of salmon. Drain liquid.

- In a small skillet, heat oil and fry salmon patties. (It will already be cooked, this is just for added flavor and texture.

- Cook noodles separately as instructed. Place noodles in bowl when ready.

- Bok choy should be soft, a sign you are ready to serve.

- Serve noodles in a bowl, pour broth over noodles and then top with corn toppings and your favorite hot sauce.

- Place salmon patties on top of ramen bowls.

- Enjoy.

Keto Shrimp Ramen with Shirataki Noodles

This recipe takes 10 mins prep, 15 mins to cook and creates 4 servings.
- Protein: 40g
- Total Carbohydrate: 8g
- Total Fat: 13g
- Calories: 300

What to Use:
- Seaweed
- Eggs (2)
- Shirataki Spaghetti Style Noodles
- Green Onion
- Minced Garlic
- Olive Oil (2 tbls)
- Sriracha Sauce (2 tbls)
- Bragg's Liquid Aminos (2 oz)
- Chicken Stock (32 oz)
- Full Shrimp (6)
- Raw Shrimp (1 lb)
- Shiitake Mushrooms (3.5 oz)

What to Do:

- Use a deep soup pan and add olive oil or avocado (your choice).

- Heat on medium high heat.

- Add the garlic first and cook until browned. Add the shitake mushrooms and the sliced green onion. Saute and then add the raw shrimp. Cook while stirring approximately 2-3 minutes.

- Add chicken broth, bragg liquid aminos and sriracha sauce and bring to a boil. Add shirataki noodles after washing and bring to a boil. Again bring to a boil.

- Divide soup into bowls and add sliced egg in each bowl. Add toppings which may include seaweed, sesame seeds, unused green onions and sriracha sauce.

Shiitake Shrimp Bowl with Cabbage and Sriracha

This recipe takes 10 mins prep, 15 mins to cook and makes 6 servings.

- Protein: 14g
- Total Carbohydrate: 53g
- Total Fat: 1.5g
- Calories: 270

What to Use:

- Lime Zest (pinch)
- Lime Juice (2 tsp)
- Peeled, Chopped Ginger (.5 inch piece)
- Chili Powder (1 tsp)
- Minced Garlic Cloves (2)
- Sriracha (1 tbls)
- Soy Sauce (2 tbls)
- Sliced Shiitake Mushrooms (1.5 cups)
- Baby Spinach (3 cups)
- Small Cooked Shrimp Peeled and Deveined (8 oz)
- Basil (2 tsp)
- Shredded Purple Cabbage (2 cups)
- Chopped Carrot (3)
- Thin Sliced Scallions (4)
- Crushed Pack Ramen Noodles (4)

What to Do:

- Cook noodles as directed, but discard seasoning packets.

- Heat shrimp as directed.

- Add veggies in a large bowl and add both noodles and shrimp to it.

- In a small dish whisk together sriracha, garlic, soy sauce, ginger, chili powder, lime juice, and zest.

- Pour the mixture over ramen and shrimp, then stir, making sure the sauce covers evenly.

- Enjoy.

Vegetarian Ramen Recipes

Simple Vegan Ramen Noodles

This recipe takes 35 mins and makes 4 servings

- Protein: 11g
- Total Carbohydrates: 57g
- Total Fat: 12g
- Calories: 372

What to Use:
- Spring Onion (2 stalks)
- Corn (150 g)
- Shiitake Mushrooms (200 g)
- Ramen Noodles (250 g)
- Bok Choy (2 stalks)
- Sesame Oil (.5 tsp)
- Soy Sauce (dribble)
- Ginger (2 inches)
- Lemongrass (1 stalk)
- Onion (1)
- Garlic Cloves (4)
- Vegetable Stock (2 liters)

What to Do:

- Cut mushrooms into slices (without the stems), as well as, spring onion and bok choy.

- Cut garlic cloves and the onion in half, peel ginger, and crush the lemongrass.

- Add veggie stock to a large pot. Bring to a boil and add your cut ingredients.

- Simmer broth for about 30 mins.

- Cook noodles separately as instructed.

- Cook until bok choy is soft and then serve in a bowl with corn toppings and your favorite hot sauce.

Spicy Garlic Tofu Ramen

This recipe take 10 mins prep, 10 mins to make and makes 4 servings.

- Protein: 31g
- Total Carbohydrates: 31g
- Total Fat: 11g
- Calories: 340

What to Use:

- Salt
- Pepper
- Basil (2 tsp)
- Crushed Red Pepper Flakes (.5 tsp)
- Sliced Button Mushrooms (2 cups)
- Diced White Onion (1)
- Crushed Chinese Noodles (4 oz)
- Baby Spinach (8 cups)
- Tofu Cubes (1 lb)
- Soy Sauce (2 tbls)
- Sweet White or Chickpea Miso Paste (3.3 tbls)
- Water (4 cups)
- Fine Grated Ginger (.5 tbls)
- Minced Garlic (2 cloves)
- Thin Sliced Scallions (4)
- Sesame Oil (2 tbls)

What to Do:

- Heat oil in a big pot. Medium heat should suffice.

- Throw in garlic, ginger and scallions until aromatic.

- Then add the water, soy sauce, and miso paste. Boil.

- Add tofu, noodles, onion. Spinach, mushrooms, pepper flakes, basin and salt and pepper to the boiling mix.

- Cover the pot and continue to cook, stirring often.

- Serve and top with your favorite toppings.

Creamy Ramen Noodles

This recipe takes 5 mins prep, 5 mins to cook and makes 2 servings.

- Protein: 11g
- Total Carbohydrates: 54g
- Total Fat: 39g
- Calories: 608

What to Use:
- Ramen Packet (1)
- Water (2 cups)
- Butter (2 tbls)
- Reduced Fat Milk (.25 cups)
- Green Onions.

What to Do:

- Boil water

- Add noodles and cook for 3 mins.

- Drain the water.

- Add butter, milk and seasoning to pot. Stir. Return noodles to pot as well.

- Cook and stir until butter is melting and ingredients have blended.

- Noodles should be coated with a creamy sauce.

- Top with sliced green onions.

Savory Vegetable Ramen

This recipe takes 10 mins prep, 1 hour to cook and makes 4 servings.

- Protein: 24.8g
- Total Carbohydrates: 64.1g
- Total Fat: 21.7g
- Calories: 537

What to Use:

- Toasted Sesame Oil with hot Chili
- Gomasio (sesame salt)
- Green Onion
- Package Baked Tofu (6 oz)
- Ramen Noodles (4 servings)
- Shiitake Mushrooms (10 oz)
- Eggs (4)
- Baby Spinach (10 oz)
- Mirin (1 tbls)
- Butter (1 tbls)
- Minced Ginger (.5 inch piece)
- Minced Garlic Cloves (2)
- Yellow Onion (1)
- Vegetable Oil (2 tbls)
- Low Sodium Tamari (.25 cups)
- Dried Shiitakes (1 oz, or 15 to 20)
- Low Sodium, High Quality Vegetable Broth (8 cups)

What to Do:

- Start by bring to boil vegetable broth and dried shiitakes in a medium pot. After cover the pot and remove the mixture from heat. For at least 30 minutes, up to 24 hours the mushroom should soak to take in the flavor of all the ingredients and when this time has passed remove the stems from the mushroom by cutting , then add 1 one cup of the broth and mushroom to blender and puree until the two have evenly blend together. Next add tamari to the ingredients and pour the mixture back into the pot. Now for a day or two the broth can be stored in the fridge and remove just before serving.

- Next, take one tablespoon of the vegetable and over a medium-high temperature, heat in a large frying pan. Continue cooking and toss in slice onion and for about 5 minutes or until they are soft and lightly browned. Remember to stir frequently, now include minced garlic and ginger and cook for two minutes and then to the pot return the mixture.

- Now hoil unsalted water, add spinach. Cook for 1 minute, then remove from pot and place it aside. Also boil several eggs, and cook for 7 minutes. After remove eggs and let cool, then peel the eggs, but be careful and make sure that no shells has been missed when peeling.. Again add water to a pot and bring to a boil, then add noodles and cook based from directions printed on the package. Drain and using four large bowls, divide the noodles evenly.

- In the same frying pan used for the onion add the remaining tablespoon of vegetable oil, and heat over medium-high as the noodles continue to cook. Mix in the sliced shiitakes along with a couple of pinches of salt. For about 10 minutes continue cooking , stirring occasionally, until the noodles reduced in volume and are lightly browned in spots.

- Arrange the ramen by rising the temperature of the broth and then remove them from the heat. Using a whisk add the butter, miso paste and mirin. After pour some broth over the noodles in bowls, just slightly to the level of the noodles. Add a small serving of spinach and shiitakes in each bowl. In each bowl place a few slices of tofu. Also in each of the bowls cut eggs in half and place two halves in each. You can also take scallions, gomasio and a little toasted sesame chili oil, with extra garnishes and serve for that little extra special taste.

Ramen with Spring Peas and Mushrooms

This recipe takes 30 mins and makes 2 servings.

- Protein: 23g
- Total Carbohydrates: 94g
- Total Fat: 6g
- Calories: 570

What to Use:

- Black Bean Sauce (2 tbls)
- Rice Vinegar (1 tbls)
- Soy Glaze (3 tbls)
- Gochujang (2 tsp)
- Eggs (2)
- Kombu (1 tsp)
- Snow peas (4 oz)
- Scallions (2)
- Cremini Mushrooms (4 oz)
- Ramen Noodles (.5 lbs)

What to Do:

- Bring a pot of salted water to a boil.

- Cut and prep veggies. Slice mushrooms, cut off ends of mushrooms, separate the white and greens of scallions and half the snow peas.

- In a big bowl, add soy sauce, black bean sauce, vinegar, 2 cups of water and gochujang to taste (spice level).

- Next, make the eggs. Fill a large pot with water, enough to fully submerge both eggs. Take the eggs and boil them for 1 min. Then remove the eggs from the heat source and place to the side, covered, for an additional 8-10 mins. When the time has completed, drain the water and let both eggs cool before processing them to be incorporated into the dish.

- Heat 2 tsps of olive oil on medium heat.

- Add sliced mushrooms. Cook 4 mins.

- Add white scallions. Add salt and pepper to taste.

- Stir for about 2 mins then add the sauce mix. Turn heat to high and boil, then reduce the heat to a medium high for 3 mins or until the liquid reduces a bit.

- Prepare noodles in boiling water, and add halved snow peas to the boiling water as well to save time.

- Cook about 3 mins then drain before adding the noodles to bowls then pouring the broth over the noodles and peas.

- Peel and half eggs, dress and serve with your favorite toppings.

- Enjoy.

Veggie Ramen with Tofu

This recipe takes 10 mins to prep, 10 mins to cook and makes 2 servings.

- Protein: 16g
- Total Carbohydrates: 30g
- Total Fat: 12g
- Calories: 350

What to Use:
- Green Onion
- Black Sesame Seeds
- Low Sodium Soy Sauce (1 tbsp)
- Oil (1 tbsp)
- Low Sodium Vegetable Broth (2 cups)
- Ramen Noodles (1 package)
- Mushrooms (2 cups)
- Eggs (2)
- Extra Firm Tofu (.5 block)

What to Do:

- Begin this recipe by fixing your typical 6 minute boiled egg. Once egg has boiled place it into a bowl of ice water then cool, crack shell and slice down the middle. Once tofu has been cut into bite sized pieces heat skillet on medium high and add tofu with sliced mushrooms.

- Saute tofu and mushrooms until light brown. Adding garlic is a nice touch, but is optional. Reduce heat and add tamari or liquid aminos and soy sauce.

- Finally, cook noodles by boiling in 2 cups of water. Use a small pot. Let noodles simmer for about 4 minutes.

- You may use remaining ingredients as toppings. This includes tofu, mushrooms, egg and veggies.

Fried Egg Ramen

This ramen recipe takes about 5 mins prep, 5 mins to make and yields 1 serving.

- Protein: 24.5g
- Total Carbohydrates: 63.2g
- Total Fat: 25.5g
- Calories: 570

What to Use:
- Black Pepper (.75 tsp)
- Olive Oil (.75 tbls)
- Pink Salt (.25 tsp)
- Teriyaki Sauce and Marinade (.75 tbls)
- Raw Kale (1.5 cups)
- Ramen Noodle Pack (1)
- Eggs (2)

What to Do:
- Boil as much water as directed on the packet of ramen.

- Once boiling, pour over the noodles in a serving bowl.

- Crack an egg into the hot bowl of water and ramen. Cover and let rest for about 3 mins.

- Add cleaned kale as well and continue letting it sit for 4 mins.

- Fry the other egg in the olive oil and add it plus your favorite seasoning to the ramen.

- Mix and stir well. Add sauce, salt and pepper to taste.

- Enjoy

Everyday Vegetarian Ramen Bowl

This recipe takes 15 mins prep, and 15 mins to prepare and yields 6 servings.

- Protein: 8g
- Total Carbohydrates: 45g
- Total Fat: 17g
- Calories: 350

What to Use:

- Toasted Sesame Seeds (1 tbls)
- Baby Bok Choy (3 heads)
- Ramen Noodles
- Large Eggs (4)
- Toasted Sesame Oil (2 tsp)
- Soy Sauce (2 tbls)
- White Miso Paste (2 tbls)
- Vegetable Stock (6 cups)
- Garlic (4 cloves)
- Grated Ginger (2 inches)
- Green Onions (5 stalks)
- Shiitake Mushrooms (.5 lbs)
- Vegetable Oil (3 tbls)

What to Do:

- Heat vegetable oil using a large pot.Now add the shiitake mushrooms and cook about 4-5 minutes. Place mushrooms on a plate and cover them with foil to keep them warm. Use the pot to make the miso broth.heat the remaining oil in the pot..Add the green onions, but only the white parts. Add ginger and garlic also. Cook about 2 minutes then add vegetable stock. Bring to a boil

- Place miso paste into a bowl and put a cup of boiling liquid and whisk until it is dissolved.Return mixture back to the pot. Cook egg and noodles by filling a large pot of water and boiling .Cool eggs by placing them in cold water . Add noodles bok choy and cook until they turn bright green. Be sure to drain. Put the noodles and bok choy in s bowl and pour some of the stock over it . Add shiitake mushrooms and eggs. For garnish use scallion and sesame.

Sweet Potato Ramen

This recipe takes about 30 mins to make and creates 4 servings.

- Protein: 8g
- Total Carbohydrates: 46g
- Total Fat: 3.5g
- Calories: 240

What to Use:

- Salt
- Pepper
- Chopped Cilantro (2 tbls)
- Hot Sauce (2 tbls)
- Sliced Scallions (4)
- Crushed Ramen Noodles (3 packs)
- Large Sweet Potato cut into cubes (1)
- Thin Sliced Carrots (3)
- Bok Choy (1 stalk)
- Frozen Corn (1 cup)
- Sliced Button Mushrooms (2 cups)
- Water (4 cups)
- Vegetable Broth (4 cups)
- Grated Ginger (3 tsp)
- Minced Garlic (2 cloves)
- Sesame Oil (1 tbls)

What to Do:

- Pour sesame oil into skillet and heat on medium low heat.

- Put in ginger and garlic and cook for about 4 mins.

- Add veggie broth and water.

- Simmer. Add mushrooms, bok choy, corn, carrots, an sweet potato pieces. Cook for 15 mins.

- Add noodles and cook for 5 mins.

- Top with scallions, cilantro, and hot sauce. Add salt and pepper to taste.

Turmeric Vegetarian Ramen Bowl

This recipe takes 10 mins prep and about 20 mins to cook and makes 4 servings.

- Protein: 7g
- Total Carbohydrates: 34g
- Total Fat: 4g
- Calories: 205

What to Use:

- Instant Ramen (4 oz)
- Hot Sauce or Sriracha
- Soy Sauce (2 to 3 tbls)
- Turmeric (.25 tsp)
- Reduced Sodium Vegetable Broth (8 cups)
- Collard Leaves (3)
- Baby Bella Mushrooms (4 to 5)
- Red Bell Pepper (1)
- Shredded Carrots (2)
- Fresh Ginger (1 inch)
- Minced Garlic Cloves (2)

What to Do:

- Combine garlic and ginger in 2 tbsp of water until softened, about 1-2 minutes, after 1-2 minutes add pepper, carrots and mushrooms. Continue to stir and saute for another minute.

- Add broth tumeric and tamari and simmer for 15-20 minutes. Afterwhich add ramen noodles and collards and stir until noodles are at desired tenderness.

- Finally, add hot sauce to taste.

Vegan Ramen

This recipe takes 30 mins prep, 2.5 hrs cook time and makes 4 servings.

- Protein: 9g
- Total Carbohydrates: 41g
- Total Fat: 14g
- Calories: 340

What to Use:

- Miso Glazed Bok Choy
- Miso Glazed Carrots
- Extra Firm Tofu (10 oz)
- Chopped Green Onions (.5 cup)
- Vegan Friendly Ramen Noodles (8 oz)
- Sesame Oil (1 tsp)
- White or Yellow Miso Paste (1 tbls)
- Dehydrated Shiitake Mushrooms (.5 oz)
- Soy Sauce (2 tbls)
- Vegetable Stock (6 cups)
- Chopped Yellow Onion (1)
- 3 inches Diced Ginger (1)
- Chopped Garlic (5 cloves)
- Grape Seed Oil (1 tbls)

What to Do:

- Use a large pot and add oil, garlic onion and ginger.

- Saute for a few minutes, about 5-8 until onion has brown edges. Add 1 cup of vegetable broth from the bottom of the pan.

- Add the broth tamari soy sauce and dehydrated mushrooms. Simmer ingredients over medium heat then reduce heat to low and cover. The longer it cooks the more flavor will develop.

- Add more sauce and sesame oil if desired.

- Use another pot to boil ramen noodles and cook according to directions.Also strain broth and reserve mushrooms for servings. When everything is ready divide ramen noodles between four serving bowls.

- Add toppings such as carrots, bok choy, green onions or tofu and serve with chili garlic sauce.

Miso Coconut Vegan Ramen

This recipe takes 10 mins prep, 25 mins to cook and makes 4 servings.

- Protein: 6g
- Total Carbohydrates: 12g
- Total Fat: 29.5g
- Calories: 329

What to Use:
- Sea Salt (pinch)
- Sweet Paprika (1 tsp)
- Tapioca (.25 cups)
- Organic Firm Tofu (14 oz)
- Black Pepper
- Spelt or Brown Rice Ramen (4 servings)
- Dulse Flakes (2 tsp) optional
- Quartered Lime (1)
- Cilantro (one-third)
- Tamari Sauce (2 tbls)
- Turmeric (.5 tsp)
- Harissa or Chili Paste (or something spicy)(1.5 tbls)
- Minced Garlic Cloves (2)
- Chopped Yellow Onion (.5)
- Organic Coconut Milk (15 oz)
- Ground Ginger (1.5 tsp)
- Chickpea Miso (2 tbls)
- Veggie Stock (2 cups)
- Slices Mushrooms (1 cup)

What to Do:

- You may or may not want to include tofu with this meal but if you do begin by mixing together tapioca with paprika and sea salt.

- Cut tofu into cubes and coat them in tapioca mix. Air fry tofu until golden brown. The next step is to make the broth.

- Once again mix the ginger, miso,tamari into vegetable stock and set aside . Preheat medium soup pot over low heat and saute the onions in water. Stir in tumeric and the harissa cook for a few minutes and add garlic. Add mushrooms and saute a few more minutes.

- Add coconut milk and let simmer. Add the fried tofu and remove from heat. Prepare pot to boil noodles.

- Boil until the noodles start to separate from each other. Careful not to overcook.. Add noodles to broth and serve hot.

- For extra taste garnish with fresh cilantro and lime wedges. Chili peppers optional.

Herb and Veggie Ramen

This recipe takes 5 mins to prep, 10 mins to make and makes 2 servings.

- Protein: 18g
- Total Carbohydrates: 92g
- Total Fat: 10g
- Calories: 520

What to Use:

- Salt
- Pepper
- Sesame Oil (1.5 tsp)
- Raw Honey (2 tbls)
- Rice Wine Vinegar (one third cup)
- Baby Spinach (1 cup)
- Thin Sliced Chives (6)
- Fine Chopped Basil (2 tsp)
- Cilantro (2 tbls)
- Chopped Carrot (1)
- Snow Peas (1 cup)
- Hard Boiled Eggs (2)
- Crushed Ramen Packs (2)

What to Do:

- Cook noodles according to packaging.

- Cook eggs until hard boiled. Peel and half.

- Add eggs, cooked noodles, snow peas, cilantro, carrots, basil, spinach and chives to a large bowl.

- In a small dish, whisk oil, honey, salt, pepper, and vinegar.

- Drizzle mix over ramen and serve.

Ramen Veggie Skillet

This recipe takes about 10 mins to make and makes 1 serving.

- Protein: 42g
- Total Carbohydrates: 15g
- Total Fat: 11g
- Calories: 340

What to Use:

- Vegetable Broth (1 cup)
- Ramen Noodle Pack of choice (1)
- Mixed Veggies (2 cups)
- Chopped Onion (1 cup)
- Oil of Choice (2 tsp)

What to Do:

- Heat oil in a skillet on medium high, then add mixed veggies and onions.

- Add broth and seasonings. Bring to a boil.

- Add noodles. Reduce to simmer and cook for about 2 mins.

- Serve.

Low-Cal Veggie Ramen

This recipe takes 5 mins to prep, 8 mins to cook and makes 1 serving.

- Protein: 5g
- Total Carbohydrates: 7g
- Total Fat: 1g
- Calories: 80

What to Use:
- Pepper (pinch)
- Ginger (pinch)
- Yeast Flakes (.25 tsp)
- Garlic Powder (.25 tsp)
- Garlic Salt (.25 tsp)
- Onion Powder (.5 tsp)
- Salt (1 tbls)
- Vegetable Broth (2 cups)
- Shirataki Noodles (1 package)

What to Do:

- Rinse and strain noodles.

- Add salt then continue rinsing.

- Pour Vegetable broth into a large pot.

- Add noodles and bring the pot to a boil.

- Combine all your other ingredients, seasonings and yeast, into a bowl.

- Add seasonings to the pot when it begins to boil.

- Cook, stirring occasionally, for 3 mins.

Vegetarian Ramen Mason Jars

This recipe takes 15 mins. to make and creates 4 servings.

- Protein: 16g
- Total Carbohydrate: 15g
- Total Fat: 3g
- Calories: 200

What to Use:
- Ramen Packets (2 packs)
- Sliced Green Onions (.5 Cup)
- Thin Sliced Mushrooms (8)
- Shredded Carrot (1 Cup)
- Baby Spinach (2 Cups)
- Sesame Oil (8 Drops)
- Red Miso Paste(4 Tsp)
- Kimchi (.5 Cups)
- Mixed veggies

What to Do:

- In 4 mason canning jars, add 1 Tsp miso paste, 2 Tbls kimchi, and 2 drops of the sesame oil.

- Boil, saute, or microwave mixed veggies.

- Divy up the rest of the ingredients proportionately.

- Add .5 of each packet or ramen to each of the jars.

- Let sit in the fridge for about an hour. Can be refrigerated for up to 3 days before serving.

- When serving, add 1.5 cups of boiling water to each jar, then close and shake. Let it stand for 5 mins.

- Add toppings if desired.

Ramen with Cauliflower and Pine Nuts

This recipe takes 10 mins to prep, 10 mins to cook and makes 2 servings.

- Protein: 18g
- Total Carbohydrates: 79g
- Total Fat: 23g
- Calories: 570

What to Use:

- Toasted Pine Nuts (2 tbls)
- Fine Chopped Basil (1 tbls)
- Salt
- Pepper
- Chili Powder (.5 tsp)
- Dried Oregano (1 tsp)
- Parmesan Cheese (3 tbls)
- Baby Spinach (2 cups)
- Olive Oil (2 tbls)
- Small Head of Cauliflower (cut into pieces)
- Packs of Ramen Noodles (2)

What to Do:

- Cook noodles as directed. Discard seasoning packets.

- Steam cauliflower over medium heat in a steamer basket.

- In a large bowl, combine the cooked noodles, oil, cauliflower, spinach, cheese, chili powder, oregano, salt and pepper. Mix.

- Serve and garnish with pine nuts.

Ramen with Almond Butter

This recipe take about 20 mins to make and creates 4 servings.

- Protein: 15g
- Total Carbohydrates: 57g
- Total Fat: 17g
- Calories: 430

What to Use:

- Chili Powder (.25 tsp)
- Sesame Seeds (1 tsp)
- Bean Sprouts (1 cup)
- Snap Peas (2 cups)
- Salt
- Pepper
- Crushed Red Pepper Flakes (.25 tsp)
- Raw Honey (1 tbls)
- Lime Juice (1 tbls)
- Ground CUmin (.25 tsp)
- Cayenne Pepper (pinch)
- Soy Sauce (1.5 tbls)

- Light Coconut Milk (1 cup)
- Creamy Almond Butter (.5 cups)
- Minced Ginger (1 tsp)
- Minced Garlic (1 clove)
- Sesame Oil (1 tbls)
- Chinese Noodles (1 lb)

What to Do:

- Cook noodles as directed. Discard seasoning packets.

- Heat oil in a large pot.

- Add garlic and ginger til aromatic.

- At this point add lime juice, cumin, cayenne, soy sauce, coconut milk and almond butter and reduce heat to a simmer.

- Mix and stir until a smooth consistency comes about.

- Remove from heat the whisk in the honey, salt and pepper, and red pepper flakes.

- Mix the almond butter dressing with noodles and serve.

Gluten Free Ramen Recipes

Chicken Rice Noodle Ramen

This recipe takes 10 mins to make and creates 2 servings.

- Protein: 86g
- Total Carbohydrate: 12g
- Total Fat: 69g
- Calories: 1040

What to Use

- Egg (pinch)
- Cayenne (hefty pinch)
- Parsley
- Fresh Veggies (.5 cups)
- Chicken Stock (2.25 cups)
- Clear Rice Noodles (2 oz)
- Shredded Chicken (2 cups)
- Salt and Pepper

What to Do :

- Begin by using a small pot to bring clear rice ramen noodles and stock to a boil.

- Cook this mixture for three minutes or until your noodles start to boil and reach desired tenderness. At this time you may add vegetables, which are optional.

- If you like a little spice in your meal add a little cayenne. You also have the option of breaking an egg into soup, stirring quickly to mix. Be sure to stir until the egg is mixed and cooked fully.

- Add chicken toward end of cooking time.

- Salt and pepper to taste.

Beef Rice Noodle Ramen

This recipe takes 10 mins to make and creates 2 servings.

- Protein: 90g
- Total Carbohydrate: 12g
- Total Fat: 72g
- Calories: 1040

What to Use

- Egg (pinch)
- Cayenne (hefty pinch)
- Parsley
- Fresh Veggies (.5 cups)
- Water (2.25 Cups)
- Beef Bouillon Cubes
- Clear Rice Noodles (2 oz)
- Serrated Beef (2 cups)

What to Do:

- Begin by using a small pot to bring clear rice ramen noodles and bouillon cubes to a boil.

- Cook this mixture for three minutes or until your noodles start to boil and reach desired tenderness. At this time you may add vegetables, which are optional.

- If you like a little spice in your meal add a little cayenne. You also have the option of breaking an egg into soup, stirring quickly to mix. Be sure to stir until the egg is mixed and cooked fully.

- Add beef toward end of cooking time.

Quick Gluten Free Ramen

This recipe takes 10 mins to prep, 10 mins to make and makes 2 servings.

- Protein: 12g
- Total Carbohydrate: 45g
- Total Fat: 4g
- Calories: 350

What to Use:

- Cucumber (half)
- Small Carrot (1)
- Thick Rice Noodle (1 package)
- Sliced Shiitake Mushrooms (5 oz)
- Coconut Oil (1 tbsp)
- Ginger (1 tsp)
- Green Onions (2)
- Maple Syrup (1 tbls)
- Tamari (.25)
- Garlic Cloves (2)

What to Do:

- Chop the veggies.

- Combine ginger, garlic and green onions with maple syrup and tamari.

- Cook rice noodles according to instructions on packaging.

- Use the coconut oil and brown the shiitake mushrooms with the sauce mix.
- Drain the noodles and combine in individual bowls with the sauce.

- Enjoy.

No Noodle Soup

This recipe takes 10 mins prep, 20 mins to make and makes 8 servings.

- Protein: 33g
- Total Carbohydrate: 4g
- Total Fat: 40g
- Calories: 509

What to Use:
- Green Cabbage (2 cups)
- Shredded Rotisserie Chicken (1.5 cups)
- Carrot (1)
- Chicken Broth (8 cups)
- Ground Black Pepper (.25 tsp)
- Salt (1 tsp)
- Dried Parsley (2 tsp)
- Dried Minced Onion (2 tbls)
- Minced Garlic Cloves (2)
- Sliced Mushrooms (6 oz)
- Celery Stalks (2)
- Butter (4 oz)

What to Do:

- In a large pot on low heat, melt the butter.

- Take dried onion, sliced veggies and garlic and put them in the pot to saute on medium heat for about 3 mins.

- Now add the broth to the pot, along with parsley, salt and pepper. Simmer until the veggies are soft.

- Add the cabbage and chicken and simmer for an additional 8 to 12 mins.

- Serve and enjoy.

Veggie Noodle Chicken Ramen

This recipe takes 10 mins to prep, 20 mins to cook and makes 2 servings.

- Protein: 29g
- Total Carbohydrate: 3g
- Total Fat: 21g
- Calories: 347

What to Use:

- Lime Wedges
- Cilantro (2 tbls)
- Spiral Zucchini (4.5 oz)
- Thin Sliced Chicken Breast (6 oz)
- Dash Hot Sauce (1)
- Rice Vinegar (2 tbls)
- Soy Sauce (.25 cups)
- Chicken Stock (2 cups)
- Ginger (1 tsp)
- Garlic (1 tsp)
- Onion (1)
- Chile Sesame Oil (1 tbls)
- Eggs (2)

What to Do:

- Place a saucer over each of the bowls to seal in the heat and let stand a couple of minutes.

- In order to enjoy this simple gluten free meal begin by using a small boiler to cut your eggs. Be sure that when boiling the eggs the water covers the eggs. After the eggs have boiled quickly place them in to cold water. Take time to peel them being mindful that these are soft boiled. Once eggs are boiled simply set them to the side until later. Next, heat the chile oil and sesame oil on high in a skillet. You will add the flavor to your meal when you add the onion, garlic and ginger to your sesame and chile oil.

- For even more flavor now add the chicken stock, soy sauce rice vinegar cilantro and for that special flavor add hot sauce.

- Bring all ingredients to a boil. Let the ingredients boil for a while then reduce heat to a simmer and add chicken breast and zucchini noodles. Again, let the ingredients simmer until chicken is cooked and noodles are tender.

- The only thing left to do is divide the noodles up between two bowls, arrange half the chicken in each bowl and do the same with the eggs.

- Spoon the broth over carefully cover each bowl with a saucer. If you can let the food stand for a couple of minutes and then enjoy!

Sriracha Non- Gluten Ramen Dish

This recipe takes 10 mins prep, 21 mins to cook and makes 4 servings. A Gluten free Faux Ramen meal is a meal to savor as a main course. Before starting this meal you may want to visit your local grocery store as some of the items may not just be available in your pantry. The first major purchase should be gluten free chicken broth and adzuki bean spaghetti.

- Protein: 33g
- Total Carbohydrate: 27g
- Total Fat: 12g
- Calories: 342

What to Use:

- Sriracha
- Fresno (1)
- Bean Sprouts (.5 cup)
- Eggs(4)
- Sesame Oil (1 tsp)
- Gluten Free Soy Sauce (2 tbls)
- Sake (.5 cup)
- Package of Dried Mushrooms
- Gluten free Chicken Broth (3 cups)
- Peeled and Grated Carrot (2)
- Slice Green Onions (4) (separate white parts and green)
- Grated Ginger (1 tbls)
- Mince Garlic Cloves (2)
- Grapeseed Oil (1 tbls)Baking Soda (2 tbls)
- Explore Cuisine Adzuki bean spaghetti
- Kosher salt (2 tbls)

What to Do:

- Once you have your ingredients all lined up begin by binging a large pot of water to boil. Once the water begins to boil add the spaghetti and cook for about 6 minutes.

- When the spaghetti is ready drain and set aside. It is time then to begin making the broth. To make the broth heat the oil in another soup pot. Cook using medium heat. Add the garlic, ginger and the white part of a green onion along with carrots.

- Cook this mixture until the vegetables are soft. This may vary based on how you prefer your vegetables. Mushy vegetables are not recommended.

- Next, add chicken broth, dried mushrooms ,soy sauce and sesame oil. You will want to cook about 10 minutes until the broth is hot and the mushrooms are tender. Add the spaghetti to the mixture and top it with peeled soft boiled eggs along with some parts of the green onions.

- Top it off with some bean sprouts, a few slices of pepper and a little sriracha to taste. This meal promises to be a new taste experience.

Gluten Free Sesame Garlic Ramen

This recipe take 10 mins to prep, 4 mins to cook and makes 2 servings. Gluten Free Ramen noodles with sesame garlic greens is a healthy meal which is very simple to make.

- Protein: 5g
- Total Carbohydrate: 55g
- Total Fat: 12g
- Calories: 350

What to Use:
- Toasted Sesame Seeds (2 tsp)
- Minced Garlic Clove (1)
- Fresh Lemon Juice (2 tsp)
- Low Sodium Soy Sauce (1 tbls)
- Sesame Oil (1 tbls)
- Shredded Carrots (.25 cups)
- Diced Marinated Artichoke Hearts (.5 cup)
- Rinsed and Chopped Swiss Chard (1 cup)
- Millet and Brown Rice Ramen Noodle Cake

What to Do:

- To cook the ramen use a large pot. Add two cups of water and place over high heat.

- Simply drop the ramen into the boiling water using a fork to separate the noodles.

- Boil the noodles for about 3 minutes. After the noodles are boiled drain them using a colander. The ramen noodles are the center of the recipe.

- Place the ramen in a large bowl and add the chards, artichokes and carrots followed by the oil, soy sauce, garlic and lemon juice which has been whisked together.

- Pour mixture over vegetables and gently toss. Place into two bowls top with sesame seeds and enjoy

Shirataki Ramen

This recipe takes 15 mins to prep, 15 mins to cook and makes 2 servings.

- Protein: 5g
- Total Carbohydrate: 6g
- Total Fat: 6g
- Calories: 217

What to Use:

- Salt and Pepper
- Shiitake Mushrooms
- Gluten Free Miso (1 tsp)
- Veggie Stock Cube (1)
- Shirataki Noodles (200 g)
- Sesame Seeds (1 tsp)
- Minced Ginger (.5 inches)
- Minced Garlic Clove (1)
- Diced Onion (1)
- Sesame Oil (2 tbls)
- Kimchi
- Baby Spinach

What to Do:

- Heat oil and add garlic, ginger sesame seeds and onion in a pan.

- Prepare the noodles as directed and then run under cold water.

- Once veggies have browned add noodles, miso, stock cube, mushrooms and enough water to cover it all.

- Turn heat to boil. Then reduce to simmer for 10 mins.

- Add salt and pepper to taste.

- Divy into serving bowls and add fresh greens, kimchi and other toppings.

- Enjoy.

Homemade Noodle Recipes

If you desire, you may use these recipes to make your own noodles instead of instant or store bought.

Homestyle Egg Noodles

This recipe makes 2 servings.

What to Use:

- All Purpose Flour (around 2 to 2.25 cups, puls additional flour)
- Egg (1) and Egg Yolks (2), lightly beaten
- Salt (just a pinch, or .5 tsp)
- Vegetable or Olive oil (1 tsp)
- Water (one -third cups)

What to Do:

- Mix 1.75 cups of flour in a large bowl with salt. Form a well in the center of the try ingredients.

- In a different bowl, add the egg ingredients, oil and water.

- Add the wet ingredients to the well in the dry ingredients and stir together until dough forms.

- On a clean surface, sprinkle flour. Then knead the dough until it is smooth and elastic in nature.

- Cover with saran wrap and let sit for 10 mins.

- Next, divy up the dough into about 4 smaller manageable clumps.

- Four your clean surface yet again and roll a dough portion out into a rectangle shape, about 12x9 inches.
- Dust both sides with more flour and let it stand for 20 mins.

- Repeat this process with each mound of dough.

- Roll the dough into a spiral, much like you would a swiss cake.

- The crosswise, maling .25 inch wide strips.

- Spread the rolls out and separate.

- Cook immediately, boiling for about 2 to 3 mins, or store for later.

- When cooking, it is best to test the noodles for doneness and stir occasionally.

- If storing (which is a good idea if you wish to make a large batch at once to use throughout the week), let the noodles dry for about and hour before placing them in a freezer bag. Place in the freezer and store for up to 8 months.

Chinese Noodles
This recipe takes 10 mins prep, 30 mins to cook and makes 3 servings.

- Protein: 11g
- Total Carbohydrate: 58g
- Total Fat: 0g
- Calories: 305

What to Use:
- Pinch of Salt
- 120 g of Water
- 250 High Gluten Flour

What to Do:

- Add flour and salt in a large mixing bowl then slowly add the water. Stir. Repeat process until there is no more flour left in the bowl.

- Knead dough. When your hands and bowl are clean then that means you are doing it right. Continue after that for another 10 mins.

- Cover the bowl with a wet towel cloth. Let it stay there for about 30 mins.

- Scatter flour on board and spread the dough by rolling it out into a paper thin rectangular shape.

- Keep the dough covered with flour.

- Fold your dough wrapper with .5cm of dough and each fold spread the surface with flour.

- Cut up the folded dough into strips.

- Sprinkle more flour on surfaces as you handle the noodles.

- Unfold them out and shake excess flour.

- Cook immediately, boiling for about 2 to 3 mins, or store for later.

- When cooking, it is best to test the noodles for doneness and stir occasionally.

- If storing (which is a good idea if you wish to make a large batch at once to use throughout the week), let the noodles dry for about and hour before placing them in a freezer bag. Place in the freezer and store for up to 8 months.

Ramen Sides Recipes

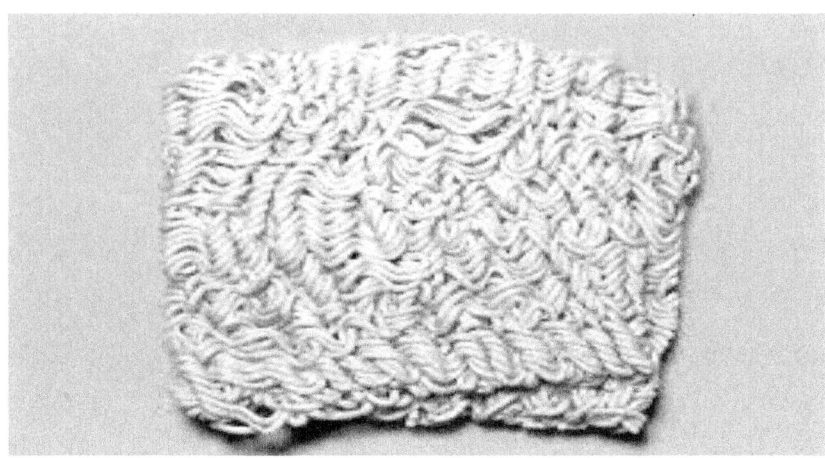

This chapter will look at recipes that go well with ramen, as well as, side dishes that incorporate ramen.

Ramen Wraps

This recipe takes 10 mins to prep, 15 mins to make and makes 6 servings.

- Protein: 24g
- Total Carbohydrate: 48g
- Total Fat: 6g
- Calories: 340

What to Use:
- Chopped Cilantro (4 tbls)
- Collard Greens or Lettuce Leaves
- Salt
- Pepper
- Peele, Fine Chopped Ginger (.5 inch piece)
- Red Chili Pepper (2 tbls)
- Minced Garlic Cloves (2)
- Sesame Oil (4 tsp)
- Cayenne Pepper (pinch)

- Chili Powder (.25 tsp)
- Raw Honey (2 tbls)
- Gluten Free Soy Sauce (3 tbls)
- Lage Cucumber (seeded, dices) (1)
- Carrots (2 shredded)
- Thin Sliced Scallions (2)
- Thin Sliced Red Radishes (2)
- Thin Sliced Green Bell Peppers (2)
- Thin Sliced Red Bell Peppers (2)
- Cooked, Skinless, Boneless Chicken Breasts, Shredded (4)
- Crushed Packets of Ramen Noodles (4)

What to Do:

- Cook noodles as instructed, but discard seasoning packs or store for later.

- Whisk honey, soy sauce, chili powder, sesame oil, cayenne pepper, garlic, chili sauce, salt, pepper, and ginger in a small bowl.

- In a different bowl, add the chicken, veggies, and noodles together in a big bowl.

- Pour sauce over the noodle mix. Stix and then spoon servings into collard or lettuce leaves.

- Wrap and serve.

Ramen Trail Mix

This recipe takes about an hour to make and makes about 6 servings.

- Protein: 14g
- Total Carbohydrate: 41g
- Total Fat: 29g
- Calories: 450

What to Use:

- Salt
- Pepper
- Chili Powder (.25 tsp)
- Curry Powder (1 tsp)
- Olive Oil (3 tbls)
- Whole Grain Cereal (1.5 cups)
- Pumpkin Seeds (.5 cups)
- Chopped Cashews (.75 cups)
- Almonds (.75 cups)
- Ramen Packs (2)

What to Do:

- Begin by preheating your oven to 400F.

- Break Ramen into bite sized pieces.

- Toss everything in a large bowl together.

- Bake on a rimmed baking sheet for about 4 mins or so, before stirring the mixture again, then continue to cook for another 4 to 5 mins.

- Remove from oven and let it cool for about 30 mins, then serve.

Ramen Coleslaw

This recipe takes about 10 mins to prep, 10 mins to make and creates 6 servings.

- Protein: 14g
- Total Carbohydrate: 66g
- Total Fat: 25g
- Calories: 520

What to Use:

- Salt
- Pepper
- Apple Cider Vinegar (one-third cup)
- Sesame Oil (.25 cups)
- Raw Honey (2 tbls)
- Sunflower Seeds (.5 cup)
- Chopped Cashews (1 cup)
- Thin Sliced Scallions (4)
- Finely Chopped Romaine Lettuce (1 head)
- Bag Coleslaw Mix (1)
- Crushed Ramen Noodle Packs (4)

What to Do:
- Cook noodles as directed but discard seasoning packets.

- In a large bowl, combine coleslaw, lettuce, scallions, cashews, sunflower seeds, and noodles.

- Mix.

- Add honey, vinegar, oil, salt and pepper in a different bowl.

- Drizzle the honey mixture over the slaw, then you're ready to eat.
- Enjoy.

Instant Pot Soft Boiled Eggs

This recipe takes 10 mins to prep, 2 mins to cook and makes 4 servings. You may also soak them in a marinade for 8 hrs for additional flavor.

- Protein: 7g
- Total Carbohydrate: 48g
- Total Fat: 13g
- Calories: 330

What to Use:

- Water (1.75 cups)
- Rice Vinegar (.25 cups)
- Low Sodium Soy Sauce (.25 cups)
- Eggs (4 to 6)

What to Do:

- Optional: Whisk together the soy sauce, rice vinegar, and .75 cups of water. (This is marinade)

- Put ice water into a bowl large enough for several eggs.

- Put 1 cup of water into the insta pot. Put in the bottom rack and place the eggs on top of that. Set on high pressure, manual. Cook for 2 mins.

- Set vent to sealing.

- Be sure to release pressure immediately and take them out after the 2 mins because you can easily cause the eggs to transition to hard boiled.

- Place them into ice water for about 3 to 5 mins.

- At this point you can be done, or you can place the eggs in the marinade you made earlier. Let it sit in the marinade for about 8 hrs.

Black Bean Ramen Pilaf

This recipe take 25 mins to prepare and makes 6 servings.

- Protein: 7g
- Total Carbohydrate: 48g
- Total Fat: 13g
- Calories: 330

What to Use:

- Salt
- Pepper
- Bell Peppers (1 cup)
- Granulated Garlic (2 tsp)
- Onion Flakes (1 tbls)
- Canned Black Beans (.25 cups)
- White Rice (1 cup)
- Beef Broth (.5 cup)
- Hot Water (2 cups)
- Ramen Noodles (2 packs)
- Butter (.25 cups)

What to Do:

- Break up the ramen noodles and cook in buttered skillet until light brown.

- Then add the water, seasoning, rice, and bouillon.

- Cover the mixture and cook for 20 mins.

- Add bell peppers.

- Stir and serve.

Corn and Basil Feta Slaw

This recipe takes 40 mins and makes 4 servings.

- Protein: 7g
- Total Carbohydrate: 18g
- Total Fat: 60g
- Calories: 630

What to Use:
- Fresh Basil Leaves (5)
- Crumbled Feta Cheese (4 oz)
- Slaw Mix (1 bag)
- Chicken Broth (.25 cups)
- Balsamic Vinegar (third of a cup)
- Sesame Oil (.5 cup)
- Ramen Noodles (1 pack)
- Dried Parsley (1 tsp)
- Butter (1 stick)
- Corn (3 ears)

What to Do:

- To get started preheat the grill to a medium-high heat, then mix the melted butter with parsley. Remember when using corn cobs be sure to stripped all the silks, and after brush each one with the butter-parsley mix. Using aluminum foil and Individually wrap the corn cobs.

- Next place the wrapped corn cobs on the grill directly over the heat and turn them about every 4-5 minutes. It should only take about 15 minutes for the cobs to be done.Please note that every grill can be different so remember to check then.

- Now it's time to mix the sesame oil, vinegar, chicken broth and ramen seasoning. When the corn cobs are ready, let them cool , then cut the corn off with a sharp knife.

- Last combine the slaw mix, corn, ramen noodles,dressing and basil in a large bowl, add the fera, toss gently and serve.

174

Pickled Cucumbers

This recipe takes 5 mins to prep, it takes 5 mins to cook and makes 2 servings.

- Protein: .7g
- Total Carbohydrate: 20g
- Total Fat: 0g
- Calories: 88

What to Use:

- Bell Pepper
- Whole Cherry Tomatoes
- Sliced Onion or Green Onion (.5 cup)
- Cucumbers (2 cups)
- Salt (1 to 2 tsp to taste)
- Sugar (optional, one third cup)
- Vinegar (one third cup)
- Water (1 cup)

What to Do:
- Combine water, vinegar, salt and sugar if you choose into a bowl. Stir.

- When the sugar and salt dissolve, add veggies.

- All the veggies should be covered in your brine.

- Let it rest in the fridge and cool and soak up overnight for better flavor.

Tamagoyaki (Rolled Omelette)

This recipe takes 5 mins to prep, 10 mins to cook and makes 2 servings.

- Protein: 15g
- Total Carbohydrate: 12g
- Total Fat: 11g
- Calories: 206

What to Use:

- Oil (1 tsp)
- Mirin (1 tbls) or Sugar (pinch)
- Soy Sauce (.25 tsp soy sauce)
- Salt (pinch)
- Eggs (4)

What to Do:

- Combine mirin, soy sauce, eggs and salt in a bowl. Mix.

- Heat a frying pan to medium heat and add oil. (There are special pans for this but a regular pan will do as well.)

- Pour a thin layer of the egg mixture into the pan until covered. Let it sit just a bit until the egg still has liquid on the top layer but has solidified on the bottom, but not too much.

- Start at one end and roll the egg to the other end forming a log.

- Add more egg to the pan until it is covered yet again. Roll again but this time from the already formed roll onto the newly cooked egg.

- Roll to the other side. Now you have one larger roll on the other side of the pan.

- Repeat this process until all the egg is used.

- Remove from the skillet and let it sit for about 4 mins.

- Slice the long into thick pieces and serve.

Onigiri (Rice Ball)

This recipe takes 10 mins to prep, 10 mins to cook and makes 6 servings.

- Protein: 16g
- Total Carbohydrate: 38g
- Total Fat: 1g
- Calories: 245

What to Use:

- Canned Tuna (95 g)
- Seaweed Sheets (1)
- Mirin (.5 tsp)
- Soy Sauce (.5 tsp)
- Bonito Flakes (.35 oz)
- Pickled Plum (1 seeded)
- Uncooked Rice (3 cups)

What to Do:

- Cook 3 cups of rice then move it from its cooking device or pot to let it cool so you can work with it.

- Deseed the plum and divide into three chunks.

- Put bonito into a mixing bowl and add soy sauce and mirin.

- Mix tuna with mayo.

- Then prepare the seaweed sheet.

- Place cling wrap over a bowl and put half cup of rice on top then place desire filling in the middle.

- Then top the other half with more rice, about half a cup.

- Wrap the cling wrap over the rice ball and form ball more coherently into a triangle.
- Cover the bottom of the rice triangle with the seaweed sheet and move to the side, repeat until through.

Eggplant with Ponzu Sauce
This recipe take 10 mins to pre, 20 mins to make and makes 2 servings.

- Protein: 1g
- Total Carbohydrate: 6.7g
- Total Fat: 7g
- Calories: 92

What to Use:

- Konbucha (.25 tsp, note: this is not kombucha the drink)
- Sesame Oil (1 tbls)
- Ponzu (2 tbls)
- Japanese Eggplant
- Sesame Oil (1 tbls)
- Shiso Leaves (5)
- Chopped Green Onions (2)

What to Do:

- In a bowl, add all the seasonings and store in the fridge until it is time to serve.

- On high heat, heat the oil and fry sliced eggplant, quarter inch thickness should suffice. Brown on both sides.

- Place on a plate or serving dish and sprinkle onions and bring out your wet seasoning dip, or dizzle it over the eggplants.

- Enjoy

Kinpira Gobo

This recipe takes 15 mins to prep, 15 mins to cook and makes 4 servings.

- Protein: 1.19g
- Total Carbohydrate: 14.25g
- Total Fat: 3g
- Calories: 97

What to Use:

- Korean Chili Thread (optional)
- Soy Sauce (1.5 tbls)
- Mirin (1 tbls)
- Sugar (1 tbls)
- Sake (2 tbls)
- Dashi (.75 cups)
- Japanese Chili Pepper (optional)
- White Sesame Seeds (1 tbls)
- Sesame Oil (2 tsp)
- Neutral Flavor Oil (1 tbls)
- Carrot (one third)
- Gobo (Burdock Root) (1)

What to Do:

- Peel the burdock root. Slice thinly in 2 inch pieces.

- Soak in water or vinegar water (with just a single drop of vinegar).

- You may need to change the water a couple of times. Do so until the water is clean.

- Leave it submerged until you are ready to cook.

- Cut carrots into similar strips.

- Fry the root by itself for a few minutes then toss carrots in the oil right with the root.

- Add seasonings and cook until most of the liquid is gone.

- Add toppings, sesame oil and seeds.

Boiled Squid in a Miso Vinaigrette

This recipe takes 20 mins prep, 5 mins to cook and makes 2 servings.

- Protein: 15g
- Total Carbohydrate: 6g
- Total Fat: 6g
- Calories: 149

What to Use:
- Japanese Hot Mustard (optional)
- Mirin (.5 tsp)
- Sugar (2 tbls)
- Rice Vinegar (2 tbls)
- White Miso (2 tbls)
- Kosher Salt
- Green Onions (3)
- Spear Squid (2)

What to Do:
- Find prepared squid from a fishmonger and have it cut into rings.

- Boil the squid until it is completely white. Cool in iced water.

- In a separate pot boil water with salt and soak the green onion at the white parts for 10 secs. Push the onion down into the boiling water fully for just a few more seconds.
- Let the onion cool then cut it up.

- Combine all the ingredients for the vinaigrette, mirin, vinegar, sugar, and miso (also hot mustard).

- Serve.

Conclusion

The world of ramen is fun and vast. Hopefully, this book gave you valuable insight on recipes and a place to start on your journey or a place to expand on your pre-existing knowledge. Use this book to your advantage. Go back and play with recipes, add or subtract. Write down ingredients that are your favorite and play with serving sizes.

This old tradition has many faces and the possibilities go far beyond just 100.

Korean Cookbook

100+ Quick and Easy Traditional Korean Recipes for Home Cooks

universal. As such, the information is given without the guarantee of its validity or interim quality.

Trademarks that are mentioned are done without written consent and can in no way be considered an endorsement from the trademark holder. This document likewise provided trademarks without written consent, and should not be seen as advertisement from the trademark owner.

Introduction

The past decade has been a boon for lovers of international food, and Korean food, in particular, has benefitted from the explosion of interest in various Asian cuisines. Many so-called "foodies" are aware of the ubiquitous Korean "taco," food truck-style, and kimchi, perhaps Korea's most famous food export, regularly appears on restaurant menus and grocery store shelves alike.

What many people may not know is that traditional Korean cooking is both easy and satisfying to prepare at home. With its warming spices and chili pastes, its generous use of garlic and fermented foods, and its welcoming traditions of many shared dishes, Korean cuisine is a justifiably renowned family friendly style of eating. While Korean food shares some elements with Japanese and Chinese cooking, its bold flavors, unique ingredients, and special traditions make it stand out in a crowded field of superb Asian flavors.

With this book, you can explore the concepts and philosophy behind the ways in which traditional Korean cooking employs its various ingredients and techniques. The idea of yin and yang—that is, balance—is very important to a Korean meal, as well as an emphasis on the five basic elements of taste: salty, sweet, sour, spicy, and bitter. In addition, the book contains explanations of basic Korean pantry staples and kitchen tools and how to use them, followed by a variety of recipes to get you started in exploring the wonderful flavors of this increasingly popular cuisine. Mashikeh-mogoseyo! Bon appetit, the Korean way!

Introduction to Korean Cuisine

Note on transliterations: Korean identifiers for items and dishes are used throughout the book with English explanation. This cookbook adheres to the Revised Romanization transliteration (though spellings can sometimes vary: "gochugaru," for example, is sometimes rendered "kochukaru").

Location: Where Korean Cooking Comes From

Warm and sustaining may be the best two words to describe the experience of eating a Korean meal. As with many great world cuisines, what Koreans typically eat is the result of geography and climate: the Korean peninsula has a climate that is similar to the North Central part of the United States, which means that there are cold winters, warm, occasionally hot summers, and extended cool autumns. This allows for a growing season wherein many varieties of vegetables and grains can be cultivated.

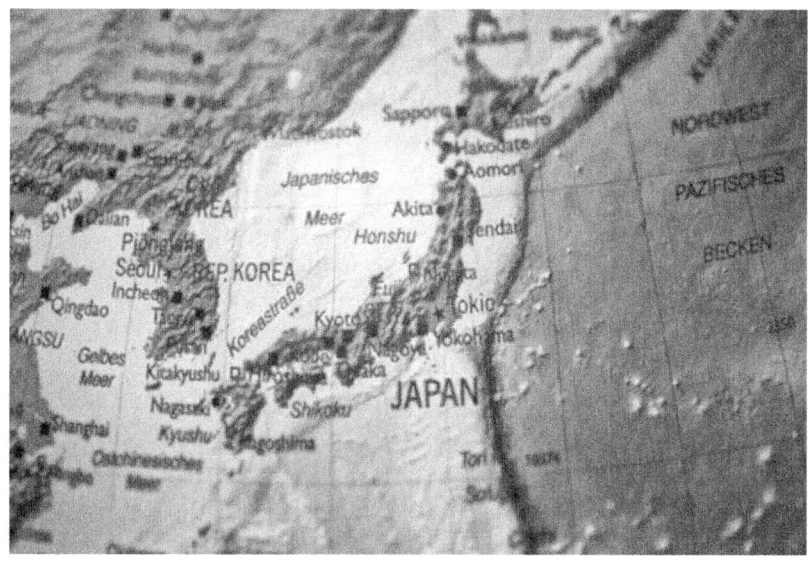

The very cold winters also create the need for preservation. Before the 20th century, Korea was mainly a rural, agriculturally based society wherein foraging and farming were central to survival for most families. Hence the need to preserve the harvest throughout the winter, often in large earthenware pots buried in the ground. This is how something like the fermented cabbage dish kimchi, perhaps the most recognizable Korean product in the United States today, comes into the story. While kimchi is readily available in Asian markets and becoming more available in general grocery stores, it is surprisingly easy to make at home with excellent results. And kimchi is merely one of a whole host of preserved, pickled, or fermented foods that play a crucial role in the distinctive taste of Korean cuisine. What once began as necessity has, with time, become a treasured tradition and an indispensable ingredient in Korean cooking. It would be virtually unthinkable to conceive of a Korean cuisine without kimchi and its siblings. See Chapter 6 for a basic kimchi recipe, as well as some other varieties of common Korean style pickles.

The agricultural traditions of Korea also give rise to the creation of hearty, robust food, food that will sustain a farmer through a long day of work in the fields or the barns and guard against the elements. Warm spices and hot chilis are ubiquitous in Korean cooking, and hearty meals include not only a main dish and rice but also numerous small plates of various foods meant to be shared (collectively called **banchan**).

See Chapter 5 for further descriptions of and recipes for typical banchan.

Korean geography also plays a key role in the development of traditional cuisine. As it is mostly surrounded by bodies of water—the Yellow Sea to the east and the Sea of Japan to the west—seafood of various kinds feature significantly in Korean food, including fish (different to each coast), shellfish, and seaweeds. Here, yet again, the tradition of preservation plays an important role in the flavors of Korean food, as many types of seafood are dried or fermented for prolonged storage. And, as with kimchi, what was once the necessity of preservation has evolved into a beloved category of foodstuffs without which

Korean food would not seem quite right. Dried sardines are served at nearly every meal, usually as a condiment to add a flavor punch of salt and funk. Dried cuttlefish is an immensely popular snack in Korea, found even in vending machines.

As you will see, the cuisine of Korea is undoubtedly unique, with its emphasis on bold flavors, hot chilis, and many styles of kimchi, with long-held traditions of sharing and respect around the table.

Yin and Yang: A Philosophy of Balance

The concept of yin and yang is familiar to almost anyone with a passing knowledge of Asian cultures. While many might immediately associate this concept with Chinese society, it is deeply ingrained within Korean culture, as well, and guides the principles of how to create a traditional Korean dish and meal.

"Yin" is associated with cooling, fresh foods, such as green vegetables and light dairy products (milk, yogurt, light cheeses). "Yang" is associated with warming, spicy foods, such as meat, chilis, and heavier dairy products. Yin food refreshes and relaxes the body, while yang food invigorates and makes the body strong. There are also "neutral" foods, as well, used to bring the yin and yang into balance. These foods provide stability and are relatively mild in taste, such as cereal grains and rice.

Cooking methods are also considered under the umbrella of "yin" or "yang." Grilling and frying, for example, are considered very "yang" ways of cooking, while poaching and steaming are typical "yin" in preparation. Foods that are left raw or fermented are also considered yin.

The idea is to create a meal that brings yin and yang into balance, with neutral foods to bind everything together. Thus, you have grilled meat, such as bulgogi (see Chapter 4 for a recipe) with some vegetable banchan (Chapter 5), fermented kimchi (Chapter 6), and rice. This balance in the meal is important in maintaining balance and health in the body, as Koreans believe, and thus eating becomes not only an act of sustenance but also an act of health and well-being.

Five Elements: Harmony of Flavors

Korean cooks also place an emphasis on utilizing and harmonizing the five basic elements of taste in their cooking: salty, sweet, sour, spicy, and bitter. This is also crucial to health, in that these five tastes in harmony can impact our organs and metabolism in positive ways. Traditional medicine often employs these concepts in nursing a person back to health, by prescribing certain foods and herbs that will assist the regeneration of certain organs (sour foods help the liver, it is thought, while bitter foods are good for the heart).

Take basic kimchi as an example. The sweetness and slight bitterness of fresh cabbage is salted to preserve it, usually with the addition of hot chili powder (<u>gochugaru</u>), and left to ferment creating a sour flavor. All five elements of taste are represented in this one dish, and as such, it has surely become the most renowned and ubiquitous Korean culinary creation.

Again, eating is more than simply to consume food out of necessity. Sitting down to a Korean meal is to engage in a sensory experience of all five elemental tastes, in harmony with the concept of yin and yang, with respect to traditional ideals of hospitality, generosity, and community.

The Korean Pantry

Below you will find a list of the most common ingredients used in traditional Korean cooking. Some of them will be familiar, while others may be new to you. For ingredients not found easily in the grocery store, try your local Asian market. Included are some suggestions for substitutions, but almost always, seeking out traditional ingredients is well worth the time and effort.

Gochugaru (Korean Chili Powder)

Gochugaru (sometimes spelled kochukaru) is the hot chili powder that is used frequently in Korean cooking. Made from dried red chilis, it is an essential pantry ingredient, especially important to kimchi. Other red chili powders can be substituted, but it must be noted that consistencies of chili powders vary widely (gochugaru is more a flake than a powder), so measurements will need to be adjusted accordingly, and the flavor will not be quite the same. Also beware of substituting American-style "chili powder," which often contains other spices in addition to the chili.

Gochujang (Korean Chili Paste)

This excellent, slightly sweet and not too spicy paste can be found at many Asian groceries and is used in a number of Korean dishes. Again, it is well worth seeking out, though it can be made at home with a few simple ingredients if you have some gochugaru on hand. This quick recipe will keep in your refrigerator for a month or more and is great to have on hand for any number of uses (tasty on most grilled foods, for example).

Method

Simply blend (in a food processor or blender) 2 tbsp of gochugaru, 2 trimmed and chopped scallions, toasted sesame oil, toasted and ground sesame seeds (2 tsps each), some minced garlic cloves, 2 tbsp of soy sauce, and a pinch of sugar, store in a container with a tightly fitted lid.

Doenjang (Fermented Soybean Paste)

This paste is made entirely from fermented soybeans and brine. Its cousin, Japanese miso, is also based on fermented soybeans but with the addition of a koji (rice) starter. Thus, doenjang is stronger in flavor in accordance with the more assertive flavors of traditional Korean cuisine.

Ganjang (Soy Sauce)

Most American home cooks are well acquainted with soy sauce. Korean soy sauce is similar to the Japanese variety most of us have in our cupboards.

Koreans also use Guk-ganjang or "soup soy sauce" which is lighter and color and milder in flavor. Be aware that soy sauces with the label "naturally brewed" are typically superior products.

Chamgireum (Toasted Sesame Oil)

Toasted sesame oil is an indispensable ingredient for any well-stocked pantry, especially for the home cook interested in Asian food. Be aware that *toasted* sesame oil is a very different product than the sesame oil you find in the aisle next to other vegetable-based oils. Toasted sesame oil is a dark amber color with a deep nutty aroma. It is most often used at the end of the cooking process lest its deep flavors are lost.

Aekjeot (Fish Sauce)

Aekjeot (fish sauce) is part of a larger group of Korean pantry staples called jeotgal, which essentially means "salted seafood."Aekjeot is commonly used to kick off the fermentation process in kimchi as well as to season various soups and stews. Also widely used in Vietnamese and Thai cooking, brands from all countries can be found in Asian groceries.

Cheongju (Rice Wine)

Korean rice wine is often used in cooking, particularly in marinades and sometimes in sauces. It is a clear alcoholic beverage with a bit of sweetness to it. Japanese sake and Chinese Shaoxing are similar products; though do not make the mistake of substituting Japanese mirin for cheongju as it is a much sweeter product. Also, be sure to use actual rice wine and not the "cooking wine" that can often be found in supermarkets; "cooking wine" is often heavily salted or otherwise diluted in order to make it legal to sell to the general public.

Ssalsikcho (Rice Wine Vinegar)

Rice wine vinegar is useful to have on hand not only for Korean cooking but also for many other kinds of cooking. It is excellent in vinaigrettes, lighter than red or white wine vinegar, and can also be used in a wide variety of marinades and sauces. Rice wine and rice wine vinegar are *not* the same product: to boil it down simply, rice wine contains alcohol and rice wine vinegar does not. And, while rice wine vinegar is less tart than its Western counterparts, it is still tarter and less sweet than rice wine.

Kkae (Toasted Sesame Seeds)

Sesame seeds can be found already toasted in many Asian markets, sometimes already toasted and ground. But you can toast and/or grind sesame seeds at home with little fuss. To toast seeds, simply heat a small pan (medium-high) and swirl untoasted white sesame seeds for about three to five minutes until they turn a light brown. If you have an electric coffee grinder, you can also grind toasted or untoasted seeds into a powder when necessary for a recipe: just be sure to clean out the grinder well before and after each different use. Or, you can invest in a separate small grinder for seeds and other whole spices.

Chapsal (Glutinous or Sweet Rice Flour)

Sweet rice flour is used in many Asian cuisines, usually in desserts. Doughs made from glutinous rice flour are sticky and elastic and have a unique mouthfeel.
See <u>Chapter 8</u> for Korean desserts using this product.

Korean Kitchen Tools

To cook good quality Korean food, the average home cook will need only to utilize whatever tools she or he already has in the cupboard. However, it is worth exploring some of the kitchen tools unique to Korean cooking and serving. These bowls and pots and utensils are indicative of Korean tradition, reminding the chef and the guest of earth and stone, of the natural world from which the elements of food and culture emanate.

Dolsot (Stone Bowl)

The dolsot is a stone bowl used both for cooking and serving. As much of Korean cooking is hearty and unpretentious, so is the dolsot. Often used in dolsot bibimbap (see Chapter 4 for a recipe), the stone can get so hot that it can essentially fry an egg or crisp cooked rice.

Onggi (Clay Pot)

These lovely clay pots are used both for serving and for storage. Large onggi are traditionally used in kimchi making, wherein the prepared kimchi is packed into the pot and buried in the ground to ferment. Onggi allows the bubbles created by fermentation to escape through its porous structure while keeping the food within fresh and free of spoilage. Until recent years, you could find buried crocks of onggi scattered throughout the countryside in Korea, and they still remain valuable and beautiful serving and storage vessels.

Siru (Earthenware Steamer)

As with the above dolsot and onggi, the siru is also a product of the earth, made with glazed and unglazed clay. It is a steamer for rice cakes and rice flour dishes, such as tteok (see Chapter 8). Historically, the siru was also used in ritual preparations of dishes for different celebrations.

Sujeo (Utensils)

This term refers collectively to the long-handled metal spoon and metal chopsticks used at nearly every Korean meal. Often, the sujeo set is carved with symbolic scenes of natural beauty, and elaborately carved sets were traditionally presented as wedding gifts. For those accustomed to eating with Chinese or Japanese style wooden or lacquered chopsticks, using the flatter metal chopsticks of Korea are a challenge initially, but their distinctive style and beauty make the effort worth the while.

Tabletop Grill

While not essential for making great Korean barbecue, the tabletop grill is a fun, innovative, and ultimately practical manner of cooking marinated cuts of meat and vegetables to order. Each diner can modify the cooking time according to his or her tastes, and the act of participating is quite enjoyable—not to mention the wonderful aromas that waft through the dining room. This method of cooking is so popular in Korea that many restaurant dining tables have grills built into the table itself. In the United States, it has become increasingly easy to find Korean restaurants who offer this kind of cooking via a portable tabletop grill, and a home cook interested in diving into the glories of Korean grilling would make great use of such a specialty tool. Bulgogi and galbi are two popular dishes that are often prepared this way (see Chapter 4 for recipes).

Rice Cooker

Most home cooks are familiar with the rice cooker. They are handy to have around not just for rice but also for steaming vegetables, dumplings, and in the case of Korean cooking, some tteok desserts. There are numerous cookers from which to choose; from expensive models that can automatically turn themselves off when sensors detect the rice is perfectly cooked to economical models that do the job well if simply. An inexpensive rice cooker is a good investment for the industrious home cook.

Korean Staples: Recipes & Guidelines for Common Dishes

Bap (Rice)

A Korean meal would hardly be Korean without rice. This staple is omnipresent, both as a simple side and as a building block for other main courses. Below are some simple recipes for Korean style rice and its many iterations.

- Prep & Cook Time: 25 min. (plus soaking, optional)
- Yield: 6 servings

Nutrition Info per serving

- Calories 225
- Fat 0g
- Carbohydrates 49.3g
- Sodium 3mg

Ingredients

- 2 cups short grain rice

Preparation

1. Wash and rinse rice in a saucepan, swishing it around in the water to release starch, at least three times. Drain.

2. Put 2 ½ cups water in a pan with rice and, if you like, soak for about half an hour before cooking (this helps rice to cook evenly and quickly).

3. Heat pan on medium-high temp, let it boil, then cover. Switch to low temp. Let rice steam for 15 minutes without removing the cover. Remove from heat, let rice stand for another 5 minutes without removing the cover. Fluff and serve.

Gukbap (Rice Soup)

Essentially, there are limitless varieties of gukbap; any soup that contains rice is a kind of gukbap. One of the most common is with bean sprouts (see below), but also visit Chapter 7 for other soups, almost all of which could benefit from a scoop of rice.

- Prep & Cook Time: 20 min
- Yield: 4-5 servings

Nutrition Info per serving

- Calories 403
- Fat 4.7g
- Carbohydrates 58g
- Sodium 1240mg

Ingredients

- 6 cups stock
- 2 cloves garlic, minced
- 2 tsps gochugaru
- 1 package bean sprouts (12 ounces)
- 2 cups cooked rice
- 1 cup chopped kimchi
- A couple of tsps sesame seeds
- 2 tsps toasted sesame oil
- 2 green onions, sliced
- 4 egg yolks (optional)

Preparation

1. Heat stock with garlic and gochugaru while you ready rest of ingredients. Blanch the bean sprouts boiling salted-water for 4 or 5 minutes then drain.

2. Divide rice, kimchi, and sprouts among 4

3. heatproof bowls, pour a little sesame oil and a sprinkling of green onions and sesame seeds. If you like, nest an egg yolk in the center of each bowl. Pour hot broth over each serving.

Juk (Rice Porridge)

Like gukbap, juk takes well to any number of ingredients (see Chapter 7 for a seafood version): a handful of chopped kimchi or other pickles; broiled or grilled meat; an egg yolk or fried egg. Below is a basic version of porridge to get started.

- Prep & Cook Time: 35 min. plus overnight soaking
- Yield: 4 servings

Nutrition Info per serving

- Calories 225
- Fat 0g
- Carbohydrates 49.3g
- Sodium 3 mg

Ingredients

- 2 cups short grain rice

Preparation

1. Wash rice in a few (3 or 4) changes of water, swirling rice around until water becomes clear. Drain a final time and add 4 cups of water to rice. Leave to soak overnight.

2. Drain rice again, and then add to saucepan with additional water (6 cups). Let it boil, put a lid, and put on medium-low. Let cook for a good 30 minutes. Serve with toppings and seasonings as desired.

Bokkeum-bap (Fried Rice 1)

- Prep & Cook Time: 25 min.
- Yield: 4-5 servings

Nutrition Info per serving

- Calories 726
- Fat 12.2g
- Carbohydrates 126g
- Sodium 525mg

Ingredients

- 3 cups cooked rice
- 2 tbsps neutral oil
- ½ small onion or 1 shallot, finely chopped
- 2-3 minced cloves garlic
- ¾ pound ground beef, chicken, or pork
- 1/3 cup kimchi, chopped
- 3 cups mixed vegetables (zucchini, bell pepper, carrot, snap peas), chopped
- Oyster sauce (about 2 tbsps)
- Toasted sesame oil (about 2 tsps)
- 2 scallions, sliced
- 1 or 2 fried eggs (optional)

Preparation

1. Have all the ingredients ready before starting. Heat the oil on medium-high in a large skillet, add garlic, onion and stir fry until slightly colored, 2-3 minutes. Add meat and stir fry until browned, about 5-6 minutes.

2. Add kimchi as well as vegetables and stir fry for another 5 minutes. Add rice then mix everything together, cooking 5 more minutes.

3. Drizzle with oyster sauce and sesame oil, and transfer to a platter. Scatter scallions over and top with a fried egg or two, if using.

Mushroom Rice

- Prep & Cook Time: 45 minutes or so
- Yield: 4-6 servings

Nutrition Info per serving

- Calories 233
- Fat 8.6g
- Carbohydrates 23.6g
- Sodium 329mg

Ingredients

- Full 2 cups rice, short grain
- Neutral oil, about 2 tbsps
- 1 white or yellow onion, chopped
- ½ pound mushrooms, sliced
- ½ pound ground beef or pork
- 1 tsp toasted sesame oil
- 2 tbsps soy sauce
- 2 tsps sesame seeds
- 2 scallions, sliced

Preparation:

1. Wash rice 2 or 3 times, then cover with water to soak while preparing rest of ingredients. Over medium-high heat, put oil in large skillet, then cook onion until softened, about 5-7 minutes. Add mushrooms and meat, making sure to break up any clumps of meat, until browned, 10 minutes.

2. Drain rice and put in skillet, accompanied by enough water to cover by ½ inch (about 3 cups). Let this simmer for 15 minutes, then test rice for doneness. If it needs more cooking time and/or more water, adjust as necessary.

3. When rice is cooked, add soy, sesame oil, and seeds, then garnish with scallions.

Bibimbap (Rice Dish with Meat and Vegetables)

This dish is perhaps one of the best known Korean dishes. It is highly versatile and an excellent platform for using leftover rice, bulgogi, and banchan.

- Prep & Cook Time: 30 minutes
- Yield: 4 servings

Nutrition Info per serving

- Calories 878
- Fat 27g
- Carbohydrates 117 g
- Sodium 615 mg

Ingredients

- ½ pound ground or thinly sliced beef
- 2 tbsps soy sauce
- 2 cloves of garlic; minced
- 3 tbsps sesame oil, toasted and divided
- 1 tbsp plus 1 tsp sugar, divided
- 1 ½ or 2 tbsps gochujang
- 2 tsps rice wine vinegar
- 1 tbsp sesame seeds
- 2 tbsps neutral oil
- ½ cup spinach
- ½ cup shitake mushrooms, chopped
- ¾ cup bean sprouts
- 3 cups cooked rice
- 4 fried eggs
- Toasted seaweed (nori), for garnish

Preparation

1. Marinate the beef in all of the soy sauce, 2 tbsps sesame oil, garlic and 1 tsp of the sugar while you prepare other ingredients.

2. Make the sauce with gochujang, rice wine vinegar, sesame seeds, and remaining sesame oil and sugar.

3. Heat neutral oil in large saute pan, then cook beef until browned, around 5-6 minutes. Add spinach, mushrooms, and bean sprouts, and then stir fry until all ingredients are cooked. (A note here: oftentimes, bibimbap is presented with each ingredient separate, as opposed to tossing together; this takes longer but makes for a prettier presentation, if desired.)

4. Mix in sauce, then divide rice among bowls, top with meat and vegetable mixture, place a fried egg on top of each serving and, if you like, garnish with nori.

Tteok-bokki (Spicy Rice Cakes)

- Prep & Cook Time: About an hour
- Yield: 2-3 servings

Nutrition Info per serving

Calories 478
Fat 3.6 g
Carbohydrates 100 g
Sodium 1175 mg

Ingredients

- 1 pound rice cakes
- 3 cups stock or water
- 3 tbsps gochujang
- 2-3 tsps gochugaru
- 1 tbsp soy sauce
- 3-4 minced cloves of garlic
- 2 tbsps sugar

- ¼ pound Korean fish cake (available in Asian markets), chopped into ½ pieces
- ½ cup chopped Napa cabbage
- 2 scallions, sliced

Preparation

1. Soak rice cakes for 20 minutes. Meanwhile, heat stock while making the sauce. Stir together gochujang, soy, sugar, and garlic for the sauce.

2. Add sauce to stock and bring to a boil. Put rice cakes into the sauce and simmer for around 20 minutes, until cooked through.

3. Add fish cakes and cabbage and cook another 5 minutes, or until fish cakes are softened. Serve hot, garnished with scallions.

BibimGuksu (Spicy Noodle Dish)

- Prep & Cook Time: 30 minutes
- 4 servings

Nutrition Info per serving

- Calories 418
- Fat 9.4 g
- Carbohydrates 66 g
- Sodium 146 mg

Ingredients

- 1 cup kimchi, chopped
- ½ cup kimchi liquid
- 1/3 cup gochujang
- 2 tsps sugar
- 3 tsps rice wine vinegar
- 1 tbsp sesame seeds
- 1 tbsp toasted sesame oil
- 1 pound somyeon (thin wheat-based noodles)
- 1 cup cucumber, julienned
- 2 hardboiled eggs

Preparation

1. Mix all ingredients up to noodles. Taste and adjust for seasonings.

2. Meanwhile, in a large pot, let water boil. Add noodles; cook until done, about 8-9 minutes. Strain then rinse under cold water, to keep noodles from sticking together. Toss with chunky sauce mixture, distribute among bowls, with ¼ cup cucumber and half a hardboiled egg on top. Serve immediately or noodles lose their texture.

Japchae (Glass Noodle Stir Fry)

- Prep & Cook Time: 45-50minuntes
- 4 servings

Nutrition Info per serving

- Calories 388
- Fat 20 g
- Carbohydrates 40 g
- Sodium 1014 mg

Ingredients

- 6 dried shitake mushrooms, soaked
- ½ pound spinach
- 3 tbsps soy sauce
- 4 cloves of minced garlic
- 2 tbsps sugar
- 2 tbsps sesame seeds
- 1-2 tbsps toasted sesame oil
- ¼ pound thinly sliced beef
- 6 ounces dangmyeon (sweet potato or starch noodles)
- 2 ½ tbsps neutral oil
- 1 carrot, julienned
- 1 small white onion, diced
- 2 scallions, chopped

Preparation

1. Soak mushrooms for 20 minutes, then stem and slice caps. In boiling water, blanch spinach for 45 seconds, then drain, let cool, and squeeze dry. Coarsely chop.

2. Make the sauce by mixing soy, sugar, garlic, sesame oil and seeds. Toss beef with 1 tbsp of sauce; toss mushrooms with 1 tbsp of sauce. Put 2 tbsps of sauce in large bowl and reserve.

3. Cook noodles in a pan of boiling water until done, about 7-8 minutes. Put in a strainer, sluice with cold water, and drain again.

4. Heat ½ tbsp oil over medium-high heat in large skillet, then stir fry noodles for 3 minutes. Transfer to bowl with reserved sauce.

5. Heat part of neutral oil in the same pan and stir fry carrot, scallion, and onion until not quite soft, about 4 minutes. Place in a bowl with noodles.

6. Heat remaining oil and saute beef and mushrooms until slightly browned for 3-4 minutes. Place in a bowl with noodles and vegetables. Add blanched spinach and toss well, incorporating and adding more sauce to taste.

MulNaengmyeon (Cold Noodle Soup)

- Prep & Cook Time: 40 minutes
- For 2 servings

Nutrition Info per serving

- Fat 4 g
- Calories 288
- Carbohydrates 46 g
- Sodium 3170 mg

Ingredients

- 1 daikon radish
- 2 tbsps salt
- 2 tbsps sugar
- 5 tbsps rice wine vinegar, divided
- 2 cups beef broth
- 2 cups chicken broth
- ¼ pound naengmyeon noodles (buckwheat noodles)
- 1 Asian pear, julienned
- ½ cup julienned cucumber
- 1 hardboiled egg, halved
- Sliced brisket or chicken (optional)

Preparation

1. Make radish pickle: cut daikon into ½ inch pieces, then mix with salt, sugar, and 2 tbsps vinegar. Set aside for at least 15 minutes.

2. Mix both broths with remaining 3 tbsps vinegar and put in the fridge for a good 30 minutes to chill.

3. Cook noodles in boiling water until toothsome, 5 minutes or so. Place in strainer and wash with cold water.

4. Divide noodles and broth in bowls, then top with pear, cucumber, and egg, and some reserved radish pickle (about 2 tbsps per serving; reserve remaining pickle for another use). If you have prepared the chicken or beef broth yourself, divide some leftover meat from cooking broth among bowls, as well.

Mandu (Dumplings 1)

- Prep & Cook Time: 1 hour
- Yield:40 dumplings

Nutrition Info per serving

- Calories 453 |
- Fat 10 g
- Carbohydrates 53 g
- Sodium 806 mg

Ingredients

- 1/2 pound zucchini, finely diced
- 10 ounces Napa cabbage, finely chopped
- ¼ pound mushrooms, finely chopped
- ½ white or yellow onion, finely diced
- 8 ounces ground pork
- 4 ounces ground beef
- 3 cloves garlic, minced
- 2 tsps ginger, grated
- 1 tbsp toasted sesame oil
- 1 tbsp soy sauce
- 1 large egg
- 1 package mandu (dumpling) wrappers (about 40)

For Dipping Sauce:

- 1 tbsp water
- 1 tbsp soy sauce
- 1 tsp of rice wine vinegar
- Scant tsp gochugaru
- ½ tsp sugar

Preparation

1. Place zucchini and cabbage into 2 separate bowls or strainers and toss generously with salt. Let sit for at least 15 minutes, then wring out excess liquid and place together in one large bowl.

2. Put everything else except wrappers into a bowl and mix together well, seasoning with a little salt and pepper as needed (about ¼ tsp of each).

3. In the middle of the wrapper, put a heaped tsp of filling, then wet one edge and fold into a crescent shape, pressing to seal edges. You can plait edges, if you like, or crimp with a fork, but this is not required. Just be sure the dumplings are sealed. Repeat until all filling and wrappers are used. (Dumplings can be frozen at this point: put on cookie sheets and freeze for an hour, then put into freezer bags for up to 2 months. No need to thaw before cooking, just add a couple of minutes to total cooking time.)

4. Make the dipping sauce by mixing all ingredients together.

5. Cook dumplings using one of the following methods:

   A. **Pan Fry**: in batches over medium-high, heat 1 tbsp neutral oil, then add about 8 dumplings, making sure they don't touch. Brown for 2 minutes, add 1/3 cup water and cover, steaming dumplings for an additional 5 minutes.

   B. **Deep Fry**: pour neutral oil (about 3 inches deep) in a large pan and get the temperature to 350 degrees. Fry dumplings in batches, about 3 minutes.

   C. **Steam**: Line steamer basket with cabbage leaves and steam dumplings in batches for 10 minutes. Again, be sure they don't touch or they might stick together.

   D. **Boil:** Cook in boiling water in batches until dumplings float, then continue to cook for about 2 minutes.

Kimchi Mandu (Dumplings 2)

Follow the cooking methods for the previous recipe to make these dumplings. Easy to make if you have prepared kimchi on hand (see Chapter 6 for recipe).

- Prep & Cook Time: 1 hour
- Yield: 25 dumplings

Nutrition Info per serving

- Calories 396
- Fat 10.6 g
- Carbohydrates 46 g
- Sodium 615 mg

Ingredients

- 1 ½ cups kimchi, finely chopped
- ½ pound firm tofu, finely chopped
- ½ pound bean sprouts, blanched and finely chopped
- ¼ pound ground pork or beef
- 6 scallions, finely chopped
- 1 large egg
- 2 tsps toasted sesame oil
- ¼ tsp each salt and pepper
- About 25 mandu (dumpling) wrappers

Preparation

1. Mix all ingredients, except wrappers, together. Fill and cook dumplings as directed in the above recipe, Mandu (Dumplings 1).

Bulgogi (Grilled Beef)

- Prep & Cook Time:15 min. plus 8 hours marinating time
- Yield: 6 servings

Nutrition Info per serving

- Calories 468
- Fat 25.5 g
- Carbohydrates 12.5 g
- Sodium 1288 mg

Ingredients

- 1 Asian pear, peeled
- 2 cloves garlic
- ½ cup of soy sauce
- ¼ gochugaru
- Toasted sesame oil, 1-2 tbsps
- 2 tbsps chopped ginger
- 2 tbsps sugar
- 2 lbs. beef tenderloin
- 2 scallions, sliced, for garnish
- 1-2 tbsps neutral oil (optional, if pan frying)

Preparation

1. Put all ingredients excepting beef in a food processor or blender and puree. Thinly slice beef and coat with marinade. (If you freeze the beef for about 30 minutes before slicing, it is easier to make neat, thin slices.) Refrigerate in the marinade for 8 hours to overnight.

2. Traditionally, bulgogi is grilled, either tableside or outdoors; however, it can be cooked over high heat in a large skillet in 2 or 3 batches, about 5 minutes per batch. Garnish with scallions.

Bulgogi Sauce

This is a nice addition to any grilled meat.
Simply mix together:

- 2 tbsps water,
- ¼ soy sauce,
- 1 tbsp each of rice wine vinegar and chopped scallions,
- 1 minced garlic clove,
- 2 tsps gochujang,
- 1 tsp sesame seeds (ground for a smoother sauce, if you like).

Daweaji Bulgogi (Grilled Pork)

- Prep & Cook Time: 20 minutes, plus 1 hour marinating time
- Yield: 4 servings

Nutrition Info per serving

- Calories 469
- Fat 27.7 g
- Carbohydrates 14.2 g
- Sodium 921mg

Ingredients

- 3 tbsps gochujang
- 1 tbsp gochugaru
- 2 tbsps soy sauce
- 2 tbsps rice wine vinegar
- 1 tbsp sesame oil
- 1 tbsp sugar
- 3 cloves garlic, minced
- 1 tbsp ginger, grated
- 1 pound pork shoulder or belly
- ½ white onion, sliced thinly
- 3 scallions, chopped
- 1 tbsp neutral oil (optional, for pan frying)

Preparation

1. Combine all ingredients up to pork for the marinade. Thinly slice pork (place in freezer for 30 minutes before slicing for easier, neater slices) and coat with marinade. Toss in onion and scallions. Leave in marinade for at least an hour at room temperature or 4 hours refrigerated.

2. Cook over high heat on a grill until caramelized and cooked completely. Alternately, heat neutral oil over medium-high in a large skillet and pan fry until done, 5-6 minutes.

Dak Bulgogi (Grilled Chicken 1)

- Prep & Cook Time: 25 min. plus 1 hour marinating time
- Yield: 4 servings

Nutrition Info per serving

- Calories 286
- Fat 8 g
- Carbohydrates 13.3 g
- Sodium 991 mg

Ingredients

- 4 tbsps soy sauce
- 2 tbsps lemon juice
- 2 tbsps sugar
- 1 tbsp honey
- 1 tbsp toasted sesame oil
- 1 tbsp rice wine vinegar
- 3 cloves garlic, minced
- 2 tsps grated ginger
- 1 tsp sesame seeds
- 1 ½ pounds chicken thighs or breasts (skinless, boneless)
- 2 scallions, sliced, for garnish
- 2 tbsps neutral oil (optional, if pan frying)

Preparation

1. Mix together all ingredients except chicken. Cut chicken into ½ inch pieces and toss with marinade. Let marinate in the fridge for an hour.

2. Grill or cook over medium-high heat in a large skillet, roughly 2 minutes a side. Be careful here, as the sugar and honey can easily burn. Garnish with scallions.

Dak Bulgogi (Grilled Chicken 2)

- Preparation& Cooking Time: 40 min. plus overnight marinating
- For 4 servings

Nutrition Info per serving

- Calories 678
- Fat 46 g
- Carbohydrates 11.5 g
- Sodium 1416 mg

Ingredients

- ¼ cup sesame seeds, toasted
- 5 minced garlic cloves
- 1 tbsp grated ginger
- ¼ cup of soy sauce
- 2 tbsps sugar
- 2 tbsps toasted sesame oil
- ½ tsp salt
- Gochugaru (optional, for a spicier version, 2 or 3 tsps)
- 1 3-4 chicken, cut into 10 serving pieces (2 wings, 2 breasts cut in half, 2 thighs, 2 legs)
- 3 scallions, sliced, for garnish

Preparation

1. Grind half of the sesame seeds (set the whole seeds aside for garnish), then combine with everything except chicken and scallions. Stir in the ¼ cup of water and mix well.

2. Make 2 slashes in each chicken piece to allow for the marinade to penetrate, then cover with marinade and refrigerate overnight.

3. Grill over moderate heat for about 30 minutes, until charred and cooked through. Turn frequently to prevent burning and watch for flare-ups. Alternately, roast the chicken in for thirty minutes at 450 degrees, turning once. Garnish with scallion and reserved sesame seeds.

Galbi (Grilled Short Ribs)

- Preparation& Cooking Time:20 minutes plus overnight marinating
- For 4 servings

Nutrition Info per serving

- Calories 1157
- Fat 47 g
- Carbohydrates 42 g
- Sodium 2200 mg

Ingredients

- ½ cup of water
- ½ cup of soy sauce
- ¼ cup of rice wine
- ¼ cup of sugar
- 1 Asian pear, peeled
- ½ onion
- 3 scallions
- 5 minced cloves garlic
- 1 tsp grated ginger
- 2 tbsps honey
- 2 tbsps toasted sesame oil
- 4 pounds beef short ribs, flanken cut (across the bone)
- Sliced scallions and sesame seeds, for garnish

Preparation

1. Put everything except ribs and garnish in a food processor or blender and roughly puree. Pound ribs to tenderize (optional), then cover with marinade and refrigerate overnight.

2. Grill until caramelized and cooked thoroughly, over high heat, about 3 minutes a side. Alternately, you can broil ribs under a preheated broiler for roughly 5 minutes a side. Garnish with scallions and sesame seeds.

Mulgogi Gochujang (Spicy Fish)

- Prep & Cooking Time: 30 min.
- For 4 servings

Nutrition Info per serving

- Carbohydrates 21.8 g
- Sodium 1065 mg
- Calories 269
- Fat 14.6g

Ingredients

- 1 tbsp gochujang
- 1 tbsp sugar
- 2 tbsps soy sauce
- 1 tbsp toasted sesame oil
- 2 cloves garlic, minced
- 4 fish fillets (such as mackerel or bluefish, preferably skin on)
- Garnishes: sliced scallions and sesame seeds

Preparation

1. Mix everything except fish together, and rub all over fish. Preheat broiler and place fish, skin side down on oiled foil placed in broiling pan (for easier clean up).

2. Broil until top is browned, keeping fish around 6 inches from element, about 8 minutes. Check for doneness but beware of overcooking. Garnish with scallions and sesame seeds.

Kkanpung Saeu (Spicy and Sweet Shrimp)

- Prep & Cook Time: 1 hour
- Yield: 4 servings

Nutrition Info per serving

- Calories 560
- Fat 5.9 g
- Carbohydrates 95.5 g
- Sodium 306 mg

Ingredients

For sauce:

- 2 tbsps each:
- Soy sauce
- Oyster sauce
- Sugar
- Rice wine vinegar
- Rice wine
- Broth (chicken or anchovy stock) or water
- 1 tbsp lemon juice

For stir fry:

- 1 pound shrimp, peeled
- 8 tbsps potato starch
- 1 large egg
- Neutral oil, for frying
- 4 dried red peppers, broken into pieces
- 5 cloves garlic, sliced thinly

- 1-inch piece of ginger, julienned
- 1 scallion, sliced
- ¼ white onion, thinly sliced
- ¼ bell pepper (any color), finely diced
- 1 mild green chili pepper (such as Anaheim), finely diced
- ½ tbsp toasted sesame oil, for drizzling

Preparation

1. Mix all of the sauce ingredients; set this aside as you prepare shrimp.

2. Devein shrimp, if you like, and mix potato starch with egg, then coat shrimp with batter. Heat enough oil in large pan to fry shrimp, in batches if necessary, and fry coated shrimp until crispy and browned, about 3 minutes per batch. Place on paper towels to catch excess oil and reserve.

3. Heat about a tbsp of oil in large pan, and then add aromatics: dried peppers, garlic, ginger, scallion, onion, bell pepper, and green pepper. Over high heat, stir fry for 3-4 minutes. Pour in sauce and bring to a boil. Cook for an additional 2-3 minutes until sauce thickens slightly. Add reserved shrimp and toss everything together well. Serve immediately, drizzled with sesame oil.

Banchan: Shared Small Dishes for Every Meal

Banchan refers to the series of small side dishes that are served with virtually every meal around a Korean table. These dishes are all meant to be shared, with a few bites of many different varieties for everyone. The more formal the meal, the more banchan will be served, typically. The following are some quick and easy recipes for Korean banchan that you can serve at home. Most banchan can be served at room temperature.

All of the following recipes serve about 4 people with a main dish or stew and white rice unless otherwise noted.

Hobak Bokkeum (Stir-fried Zucchini)

- Prep & Cook Time: 15 min.

Nutrition Info per serving

- Calories 58
- Fat 5g
- Carbohydrates 2.8g
- Sodium 353mg

Ingredients

- 1 medium zucchini
- 1 tbsp neutral oil, such as canola
- 2 cloves of garlic, minced
- 3 tsps fish sauce
- 1 tsp toasted sesame oil
- 1 scallion, minced
- 1 tsp sesame seeds, preferably toasted

Preparation

1. Slice zucchini in half lengthwise, then in ¼ inch slices crosswise, to create half-moons.

2. Heat tbsp of oil over medium-high heat in saute pan. Toss in zucchini, garlic, and fish sauce and cook for 4 minutes.

3. Stir in the sesame oil, scallion, and 2 tbsps of water and continue cooking for another 2 minutes, until zucchini softens.

4. Sprinkle with sesame seeds and serve.

- Prep & Cook Time: 20 min.

Nutrition Info per serving

- Calories 29
- Fat 5 g
- Carbohydrates 11 g
- Sodium879mg

Ingredients

- 3 Kirby cucumbers or 1 English cucumber
- 1 ½ tsps salt
- 3 tsps neutral oil
- 1 minced clove garlic
- 1 minced scallion
- 1 tsp each of toasted sesame oil and sesame seeds

Preparation

1. Cut the cucumbers into half-moon shapes (no need to de-seed them if using Kirby or English cucumber). Toss with salt and let sit for at least 5 minutes in a strainer. Squeeze dry before continuing.

2. Heat neutral oil on medium-high temp, toss in cucumbers, garlic, and scallion and stir fry for 2 minutes.

3. Off heat, sprinkle with sesame oil and seeds.

Gaji Bokkeum (Stir-fried Eggplant)

- Prep & Cook Time: 15 min.

Nutrition Info per serving

- Calories 136
- Fat 10 g
- Carbohydrates 12 g
- Sodium 262 mg

Ingredients

- 2 medium Asian eggplants (small and slender, not large globe eggplants)
- 3 mild green chili peppers or half a green bell pepper
- 2 tbsps neutral oil
- ½ tbsp gochujang
- 1 tbsp rice wine
- 1 tbsp soy sauce
- 2 cloves garlic, minced
- 1 tsp. sugar
- 2 tsps toasted sesame oil
- 1 tsp. sesame seeds

Preparation

1. Cut eggplants into half moons and cut chili peppers into slim rounds (1/2 inch pieces if using bell pepper).

2. Heat oil (medium-high heat) in saucepan and add eggplant and peppers. Stir fry for 2 minutes, or until the eggplant softens, add all remaining ingredients except sesame oil and seeds. Stir fry until eggplant is cooked and the peppers wilt roughly 5 minutes.

3. Sprinkle with sesame oil and seeds and serve.

Myulchi Bokkeum (Stir-fried Anchovies)

- Prep & Cook Time: 20 min.

Nutrition Info per serving

- Calories 195
- Fat 18.8 g
- Carbohydrates 3,7 g
- Sodium 638 mg

Ingredients

- 1 cup dried anchovies
- 3 tbsps neutral oil
- 1 minced clove garlic
- 1 tbsp sugar
- 2 tbsps toasted sesame oil
- 2 tsps gochujang
- 1 tbsp soy sauce
- 1 tsp sesame seeds

Preparation

1. Soak anchovies in water for about 10 minutes.

2. Put oil in skillet and heat on medium. Drain and add anchovies to oil. Saute until browned and crisp, about 8 minutes.

3. Add rest of ingredients except sesame seeds and saute another 2 minutes for flavors to meld. Adjust seasonings to taste, then transfer anchovies to paper towels to drain and sprinkle with sesame seeds.

Buchimgaeor Jeon (Korean Pancakes)

The terms buchimgae and jeon refer to cooking a variety of ingredients in a pancake-like batter. These can be made with meat, seafood, or vegetables. Below are a few recipes for vegetable-centered buchimgae.

Kimchi Buchimgae (Kimchi Pancake)

- Prep & Cooking Time: 25 min.
- Yield: 4 large pancakes

Nutrition Info per serving

- Calories 166
- Fat 10 g
- Carbohydrates 31.9 g
- Sodium 352 mg

Ingredients

- 2 ½ cups each: all-purpose flour and water
- 1 large egg
- 2 cups kimchi, coarsely chopped
- 1 tbsp kimchi pickling liquid
- Some neutral oil
- 2 or 3 green or red chilis, sliced (optional)
- Sliced scallions for garnish

Preparation

1. Whisk together flour, water, and egg, then stir in kimchi and kimchi liquid to the mix. Throw in a few ice cubes to keep batter cold while heating pan.

2. Heat about 1 tbsp oil over high heat in a nonstick pan, then add ¼ of batter. Sprinkle chilis over, if using. Cook for about 1 minute, then place on medium-low heat and cook until bottom is done and edges start to cook about 4-5 minutes.

3. Flip pancake and cook another 4-5 minutes. Slide out of the pan, cut into wedges or squares and garnish with scallions. Repeat with remaining ingredients.

Pajeon (Scallion Pancake)

- Prep & Cook Time: 15 min.
- Yield: Makes 2 pancakes

Nutrition Info per serving

- Calories 242
- Fat 15 g
- Carbohydrates 22 g
- Sodium307 mg

Ingredients

- ¾ cup each: all-purpose flour and ice water
- 2 tbsps cornstarch
- 1 minced clove garlic
- ½ tsp salt
- 1 lightly beaten egg
- 1 bunch scallions, trimmed, halved if thick
- 4 tbsps neutral oil

Preparation

1. Mix together flour, cornstarch, garlic, salt, ice water and half of the beaten egg. Thin the batter with some more water to create the consistency of thick cream, if necessary.

2. Heat 2 tbsps oil over medium heat in a nonstick pan, then pour half the batter into the pan and immediately lay half the scallions on top of the batter. Drizzle with half the remaining beaten egg and cook for 4 minutes.

3. Turn pancake over and cook for another 3-4 minutes. Repeat with remaining ingredients.

Hobak Buchimgae (Zucchini Pancakes)

- Prep & Cook Time: 30 min.
- Yields: 2 pancakes

Nutrition Info per serving

- Calories 191
- Fat 14 g
- Carbohydrates 14.7 g
- Sodium 50 mg

Ingredients

- 1 medium zucchini, cut into matchstick shapes
- Salt
- 1 shallot, thinly sliced
- 2 green chili peppers, such as serranos, thinly sliced and seeded
- 6 tbsps flour
- 2 tbsps cornstarch
- 1 large egg
- 4 tbsps neutral oil

Preparation

1. Toss the zucchini with about ½ tsp of salt and set aside in a bowl for 12 minutes. Squeeze well, reserving liquid in the bowl, and set zucchini aside.

2. Add flour, cornstarch, and egg to bowl with zucchini liquid and mix together well. Stir in the zucchini, shallot, and chili peppers. If the mixture is too thick, add another couple of tbsps of water.

3. Heat 2 tbsps oil over medium heat in nonstick pan. Spoon in half of the batter mixture and cook for about 5 minutes each side. Repeat with remaining oil and batter.

Gamja Jeon (Potato Pancakes)

- Prep & Cook Time: 30 min.
- Yields: 6 small pancakes

Nutrition Info per serving

- Calories 150
- Fat 11.7 g
- Carbohydrates 11 g
- Sodium 200 mg

Ingredients

- 2 medium baking potatoes, peeled
- ½ medium white or yellow onion, peeled
- ½ tsp salt
- 1 green chili pepper, sliced (optional)
- 1 scallion, sliced (optional)
- 4 tbsps neutral oil

Preparation

1. Puree the potatoes in a food processor or blender, then spoon into a strainer over a bowl and let sit for about 5 minutes.

2. Meanwhile, puree the onion and pour into another bowl, then add the strained potato to this with the salt.

3. Stir in reserved potato liquid until the mixture reaches a batter-like consistency.

4. Heat 2 tbsps oil in nonstick pan and make 3 small pancakes

with half the batter. Top each with some sliced chili and/or scallion and cook for roughly 5 minutes a side, so the cake is browned and crisp. Repeat with remaining oil and batter.

Pancake Dipping Sauce

Korean pancakes are typically served with a basic soy dipping sauce. To make, combine equal parts soy sauce, water, and rice vinegar and half part sugar (so, for example, 4 tbsps soy, water, vinegar to 2 tbsps sugar). The sauce can be enhanced with any number of flavors should you wish to embellish: add some sliced scallion and/or minced garlic for pungency; thinly sliced green or red chili or some gochugaru for heat; and/or some toasted sesame oil or sesame seeds for nuttiness.

Namul (Vegetables)

<u>This category of banchan side dishes</u> broadly refers to fresh greens, vegetables, and herbs often made with seasonal ingredients.

While typically steamed or blanched before seasoning, namul can also be boiled or fried or served raw.

Below are some recipes for common namul dishes, but use your imagination and your own seasonal ingredients to tailor these recipes to your tastes and locale.

Kongnamul Muchim (Seasoned Bean Sprouts)

- Prep & Cook Time: 10 min.

Nutrition Info per serving

- Calories 72
- Fat 4 g
- Carbohydrates 5.9 g
- Sodium 590 mg

Ingredients

- 1 pound of bean sprouts
- 1 tsp salt
- 2 minced scallions
- 2 minced cloves garlic
- 1 tbsp toasted sesame oil
- 1 tsp.sesame seeds
- Salt to taste
- 1-2 tsps gochugaru (optional, for a spicier version)
- 1 tbsp soy sauce (optional, for a spicier version)

Preparation:

1. Make sure sprouts are washed, then place in a saucepan with a tightly fitting lid and add 1 tsp salt and 1 cup water. Cover and cook over high heat, undisturbed, for 6-7 minutes.

2. Drain well and quickly plunge into a bowl of ice water (this process, known as shocking, stops the cooking process and maintains texture and color). Drain, then toss with the remaining ingredients and serve.

Sigeumchi Namul (Blanched Spinach)

- Prep & Cook Time: 20 min.

Nutrition Info per serving

- Calories 40
- Fat 1.9 g
- Carbohydrates 4.7 g
- Sodium 143 g

Ingredients

- 1 bunch spinach, cleaned, 10-12 ounces
- 2 cloves minced garlic
- 1-2 minced scallions
- ½ tsp sugar
- 1 tsp each: soy sauce, toasted sesame oil, and sesame seeds
- 2 tsps gochujang (optional, for a spicier version)
- Additional tsp soy sauce (optional, for a spicier version)

Preparation

1. Blanch spinach in boiling water, lightly salted, for about 45 seconds, then drain and shock in a bowl of ice water.

2. Let cool, then drain and squeeze out excess water. Chop spinach roughly, then add remaining ingredients. Let meld for about 10 minutes for optimum flavor.

Gaji Namul (Steamed Eggplant)

- Prep & Cook Time: 15 min.

Nutrition Info per serving

- Calories 70
- Fat 2.9 g
- Carbohydrates 10.6 g
- Sodium 456 mg

Ingredients

- 2 medium Asian eggplants cut into 2-inch batons
- 2 minced cloves garlic
- 2 scallions, minced
- 2 tbsps soy sauce
- 2 tsps toasted sesame oil
- ½ tsp sugar
- ½ tsp gochugaru
- 1 tsp sesame seeds

Preparation

1. Steam eggplant until tender but not mushy, about 3-5 minutes.

2. Let cool slightly, toss with remaining ingredients.

- Prep & Cook Time: 15 min.

Nutrition Info per serving

- Calories 22
- Fat 1.6g
- Carbohydrates 1.3g
- Sodium 12mg

Ingredients:

- 2 bunches watercress (about 12 ounces)
- 2 minced scallions
- 2 minced cloves garlic
- 1 tsp each toasted sesame oil and sesame seeds Salt to taste

Preparation

1. Blanch trimmed and cleaned watercress in boiling, salted water for 45 seconds. Shock in a bowl of ice water and drain when cool.

2. Squeeze excess water out of cress, chop, and toss with remaining ingredients.

- Prep & Cook Time: 15 min.

Nutrition Info per serving

- Calories 90
- Fat 6.3 g
- Carbohydrates 8.2 g
- Sodium 328 mg

Ingredients

- 2 large daikon radish, peeled
- 1 tbsp neutral oil
- 2 minced cloves garlic
- 2 scallions, minced
- 2 tsps toasted sesame oil
- 1 tsp sesame seeds

Preparation

1. Cut the radish into matchsticks.

2. Over medium-high, heat oil, stir fry the radish with ½ tsp salt and garlic for roughly 5 minutes.

3. Add 3 tbsps of water, turn down to medium-low, and cover. Continue cooking until radish is tender, another 3 minutes.

4. Add garlic, scallions, sesame oil and seeds, toss, and serve.

Other Banchan

There are many other categories of banchan, as well, such as hoe (raw or lightly blanched seafood), jorim (simmered dishes), muk (grain porridges), pyeonyuk (boiled and pressed meat), po (dried meat), seon (stuffed dishes), and ssam (wrapped dishes). See below for a variety of other types of banchan to round out your Korean meal.

- Prep & Cook Time: 45 min. plus 6 hours soaking time

Nutrition Info per serving

- Calories 264
- Fat 9.3 g
- Carbohydrates 28.4 g
- Sodium 968 mg

Ingredients

- 1 cup dried soybeans (yellow or black)
- 4 tbsps soy sauce
- 2 tbsps sugar
- 2 tbsps of rice wine
- 1 tbsp corn syrup

Preparation

1. Soak the dried beans for 6 hours. Drain.

2. Put beans with 2 cups water in a pot and let come to a boil for 5 minutes, then skim the surface of any foam.

3. Add soy, sugar, and rice wine and lightly boil for about 30 minutes, uncovered, allowing the beans to absorb the sauce.

4. Add the corn syrup at the very end of cooking, and stir to coat. This can be served immediately or at room temperature, sprinkled with sesame seeds if desired.

Gamja Jorim (Braised Potatoes)

- Prep & Cook Time: 30 min.

Nutrition Info per serving

- Calories 214
- Fat 5.2g
- Carbohydrates 40g
- Sodium 731mg

Ingredients

- 3 medium potatoes, peeled
- ½ green bell pepper
- 1 carrot, peeled
- ½ white onion
- 1 tbsp sugar
- 3 tbsp soy sauce
- 1 tbsp rice wine
- 2 minced cloves garlic
- 1 tbsp honey
- 1 tbsp neutral oil
- 1 tsp each toasted sesame oil and sesame seeds

Preparation

1. Cut the vegetables into 1-inch pieces. Mix soy, sugar, rice wine, garlic, honey and ½ cup of water in a bowl.

2. Heat tbsp oil in a pan and cook potatoes and carrot for about 5 minutes. Add sauce and heat to a boil, then cover and lower heat, cooking until potatoes are tender, roughly 7 minutes.

3. Toss in onion, bell pepper and simmer uncovered for another 5 minutes. Drizzle with sesame oil and seeds and serve.

Dubu Jorim (Braised Tofu)

- Prep & Cook Time: 25 min.

Nutrition Info per serving

- Calories 147
- Fat 11.6 g
- Carbohydrates 4.6 g
- Sodium 461 mg

Ingredients

- 1 pound soft tofu
- 2 tbsp neutral oil
- 2 tbsp soy sauce
- 1 tsp gochugaru
- 1 minced clove garlic
- 2 minced scallions
- 1 tsp sugar
- 1 tsp sesame seeds
- ¼ water

Preparation

1. Cut tofu into ½ inch thick slices. On a skillet, heat oil over medium-high heat and fry tofu, turning once, until slightly browned, about 2 minutes a side.

2. Mix together remaining ingredients and pour over tofu. Cover pan, decrease heat to low and cook for about 10 minutes, so tofu is cooked and coated with sauce. Transfer tofu to plate and drizzle with sauce.

Oi Muchim (Cucumber Salad)

- Prep & Cook Time: 20 min.

Nutrition Info per serving

- Calories 42
- Fat 1.7 g
- Carbohydrates 6.7 g
- Sodium 585 mg

Ingredients

- 2 Kirby cucumbers or 1 English cucumber
- 1 minced clove garlic
- 1 scallion, minced
- 1 tbsp gochugaru
- 1 tsp of rice wine vinegar
- ½ tsp sugar
- 1 tsp each toasted sesame oil and sesame seeds

Preparation

1. Cut cucumbers into rounds (no need to de-seed if using English cucumber). Rub 1 tsp. salt into rounds and let sit for 15 minutes.

2. Drain well and mix in all other ingredients.

- Prep & Cook Time: 30 min.

Nutrition Info per serving

- Calories 29
- Fat .5g
- Carbohydrates 5.8g
- Sodium 833mg

Ingredients

- 1 large daikon radish, peeled
- 3 minced cloves garlic
- 3 scallions, minced
- 2 tbsp gochugaru
- 2 tsps fish sauce
- ½ tsp sugar
- 1 tsp sesame seeds

Preparation

1. Cut daikon into matchsticks and sprinkle with 1 tsp. salt, rubbing in well. Let sit for about 20 minutes, then drain off excess liquid.

2. Mix with remaining ingredients. Check for seasoning, and dash with more fish sauce if necessary.

- Prep & Cook Time: 40 min.

Nutrition Info per serving

- Calories 52
- Fat 3 g
- Carbohydrates 4.8 g
- Sodium 137 mg

Ingredients

- 1 head Napa Cabbage
- 1-2 tbsp doengjang
- 2 tsps toasted sesame oil
- 1 tsp. sesame seeds

Preparation

1. Bring salted water to a boil in a pot. Remove tough core of cabbage, and separate cabbage into leaves. Boil until white part of cabbage is tender, about 5 minutes.

2. Drain and shock in ice water to halt cooking. Squeeze excess liquid out of cabbage leaves.

3. Cut cabbage into 2-inch lengths and toss with remaining ingredients. Let meld for at least 20 minutes before serving.

- Prep & Cook Time: 45 min.

Nutrition Info per serving

- Calories 238
- Fat 7.9g
- Carbohydrates 41g
- Sodium 10mg

Ingredients

- 1 pound sweet potatoes
- Neutral cooking oil (for frying) + 1 tbsps
- 3 tbsp sugar
- 2 tsps sesame seeds

Preparation

1. Peel and cut sweet potatoes into ½ inch chunks. Soak in cold water to remove excess starch, about 30 minutes. Draw off water and dry well.

2. Heat enough oil in large skillet to cover potatoes. The oil should register 350 before adding sweet potatoes.

3. Fry sweet potatoes until cooked through, about 7 minutes, then transfer with slotted spoon to paper towels or a brown paper bag to drain off oil.

4. Put the final tbsp of oil in a saute pan and stir in the sugar. Cook over medium-high until sugar melts and starts to caramelize. Turn heat to low and add cooked drained sweet potatoes. Toss well with sauce then garnish with sesame seeds.

- Prep & Cook Time: 30 min.

Nutrition Info per serving

- Calories 130
- Fat 7.5 g
- Carbohydrates 5.7 g
- Sodium 1074 mg

Ingredients

- 6 large eggs, hard boiled
- 2 tbsp of rice wine
- 4 tbsp soy sauce
- 1 shallot or fat green onion

Preparation

1. Peel the eggs. Add all other ingredients to the saucepan along with a cup of water and raise to a boil.

2. Add eggs to saucepan, lower the heat, and simmer for about 15 minutes so the sauce is reduced by half. Roll the eggs around during cooking so that entire egg gets coated in sauce.

3. Cool eggs, slice and serve at room temperature or cold.

GimGui (Toasted Seaweed)

- Prep & Cook Time: 5 min.

Nutrition Info per serving

- Calories 43
- Fat 4g
- Carbohydrates 0g
- Sodium5mg

Ingredients

- 8 sheets of dried seaweed (often found under their Japanese name, nori)
- 1 tsp toasted sesame oil
- 1 tbsp neutral oil
- Salt

Preparation

1. Arrange sheets shiny side up. Mix oils in a small bowl and brush shiny side with oil. Salt lightly.

2. Place under the broiler for 5-10 seconds, being careful not to let sheets burn. Alternatively, suspend over a gas flame, rotating to cook evenly

3. Let cool, then cut into squares. Makes for a nice snack, as well.

Ssamjang (Dipping Sauce)

While not actually a banchan side dish, ssamjang is a frequent accompaniment to Korean meals, as the most renowned dipping sauce for a wide variety of foods, particularly grilled meats (see Chapter 4). It can be bought pre-made but is also easy to make at home if you've stocked your Korean pantry well.

Mix together

- ¼ cup doenjang with 1-2 tbsp of gochujang, according to your preferred spice level.

- Add minced garlic clove and a couple of minced scallions, 2 tsps each of honey and toasted sesame oil, and 1 tsp sesame seeds.

Kimchi and Other Pickles

The significance of kimchi to Korean cuisine cannot be overstated. Some form of kimchi is served with nearly every meal of every type. It would not be an overstatement to suggest that kimchi is the national dish of Korea. While you can purchase kimchi in Asian markets and some grocery stores, it is fairly simple and very satisfying to make at home. All it takes is patience! What follows here are some traditional recipes for making kimchi, adjusted for the home cook, as well as some shortcuts for quicker pickles to make and eat that day.

Kimchi

Traditional Cabbage Kimchi
- Prep Time: 1 hr.
- Total Time: 12 hrs. plus fermentation time 3-6 days
- Yields: about 1 ½ quart

Ingredients

- 2 pounds Napa cabbage, cut into roughly 2-inch pieces
- 6 scallions, chopped finely or slivered
- 6 minced cloves of garlic
- 1 ½ tbsp fresh ginger, peeled and minced
- 2 tbsps gochugaru (or other red chili powder but with caution)
- 1 or 2 tsps of sugar

Preparation

1. Make brine with 3 tbsp of salt and 6 cups of water.

2. Place chopped cabbage in a large bowl or nonreactive pot (or, if you've been industrious with shopping, a Korean <u>onggi</u>) and ladle brine over cabbage. Weigh down with something (plate, platter) to keep the cabbage submerged and let this sit out for 12 hours.

3. Now remove cabbage, but reserve the brine. Toss cabbage with a tsp of salt and all else remaining. Pack this mixture into a 2-quart jar (or, alternatively, 2 1 quart jars: old, washed mayonnaise jars work) and pour brine over just to cover.

4. Take a freezer or sandwich storage bag and push it into the mouth of the jar. Pour remaining brine into the bag and seal it; this keeps the cabbage submerged in the brine while allowing the bubbles caused by fermentation to escape. (If the jar is sealed, it could shatter from the pressure released during fermentation.)

5. Allow the kimchi to ferment in a cool place, ideally around 68 degrees (a garage in cool weather works, or an inner closet during warmer weather), for about 3-6 days. It will get sourer as time passes.

6. Remove the bag with brine and seal your jar tightly. Your kimchi should keep in the refrigerator for months.

- Prep Time: 20-25 min. Brining time: 48 hours.
- Yields: 1 ½ quart

Ingredients

- Napa cabbage, head, sliced into 1-inch squares
- 2 tbsp sugar
- 2 tbsp kosher or sea salt
- 10 cloves of garlic, minced
- 10 scallions, minced
- 2 tbsp of grated ginger
- ¼-1/2 cup gochugaru (more chili powder yields hotter kimchi)
- ¼ soy sauce
- ¼ fish sauce (optional but it does mimic the fermented flavor of the more traditional recipe)

Preparation

1. Toss the cabbage with the sugar and salt in a nonreactive container; rub seasonings in well. Refrigerate overnight.

2. The next day mix together the remaining ingredients, adding water if the brine is too thick; it should have the consistency of a creamy-style salad dressing. Drain the cabbage and add it to your briny mixture.

3. Pack into the jar(s) and refrigerate. It will be good in another 24 hours but even better as it absorbs flavors over time.

Kkaekdugi (Radish Kimchi)

Follow the previous recipe, substituting three medium daikon radishes (large white radishes, available in most grocery stores). Be sure to peel them and cut into ½ inch chunks. Radish kimchi is excellent in hearty stews, bringing a satisfying sour crunch to balance the richness of the stew.

Baek-kimchi (Chili free Kimchi or "White Kimchi")

This kimchi is good for those with a low tolerance for heat (such as younger children). It is a light somewhat sweet pickle with just a touch of fermented flavor. If you want to up the funky flavor, add 2-4 tbsp of fish sauce to the brine.

- Prep Time: about 2hrs, largely unattended.
- Brining time: 3 days
- Yields: 1 ½ quart

Ingredients

- 1 Napa cabbage, quartered
- ¼ cup kosher or coarse sea salt dissolved in 4 cups water

Puree:

- 1 tbsp kosher or coarse sea salt
- 1 Asian or Bosc pear, peeled and cored
- 1 small red apple, peeled and cored
- 1 large or 2 small shallots
- 3 minced cloves garlic
- 1 tsp grated ginger
- 4 cups of water

Preparation

1. Soak the cabbage quarters in the brine, weighed down with a plate, for about 1 ½ hour. Drain well.

2. Meanwhile, puree the additional water and salt, pear, apple, shallot, garlic, and ginger in a food processor or blender. Push this mixture through a fine sieve to remove coarse food particles, toss with cabbage quarters. Cover loosely, then leave at cool room temperature for 12-24 hours to ferment.

3. Transfer to the refrigerator for another 3-7 days (it gets sourer as you leave it). This kimchi does not keep as long as others, about two weeks.

Dongkimchi (Winter Kimchi)

- Prep Time: 1 hr.
- Brining time: 2 hrs.plus 2 days to 2 weeks
- Yields:1 ½ quart

Ingredients

- ½ Napa cabbage, chopped into 2-inch pieces
- 2 daikon radishes, chopped into 1-inch pieces
- 3 tbsp coarse salt
- 1 tbsps sugar
- 1 small Asian pear, peeled and cored
- 1-inch piece of ginger
- 5 cloves of garlic
- 1 shallot
- 2-3 red or green chilis, slivered
- 2 scallions, slivered

Preparation

1. Make a brine for the cabbage with 2 tbsp salt and 1 cup of water. Combine and let stand, weighted down with a plate, for a couple of hours.

2. Toss the radish pieces with a tbsp of salt and the sugar and set aside for 30 minutes.

3. Drain both cabbage and radish well, rinsing off excess salt if you like, though it should remain a bit salty. Reserve the brine from cabbage and any liquid exuded by radishes.

4. Puree pear, garlic, ginger and shallot with ½ cup of water;

strain this, if desired, then add to reserved brine.

5. Toss cabbage and radish with chilis and scallions, pack into the jar(s) and pour seasoned brine over. If you need more brine to cover, mix 2 tbsp of salt with an additional 4 cups of water, and use this to cover.

6. Leave dongkimchi out at cool room temp for two days then put in refrigerator for another 2 weeks. It is ready to eat any time after the initial 2 days but gets more complex with time. This keeps for a couple of months.

Nabak-kimchi (Spring Kimchi)

Spring kimchi is very similar to winter kimchi, with the addition of some carrot for a different flavor and more color (1-2 small carrots, slivered). Both winter and spring kimchis are often prepared with slurry made from rice flour and water; this gives the "water kimchi" a bit of body and a touch of sweetness. If you like, mix 1 tbsp of sweet rice flour with a cup of water and add this along with the brine mixture in Step 5 in the previous recipe.

Oisobagi (Cucumber Kimchi)

- Prep Time: 30-40 min.
- Brining: 15 min. to 2 weeks
- Yields: 1 quart

Ingredients

- 1 pound Kirby cucumbers (small unwaxed cucumbers), cut into ½ inch spears
- 1 ½ tsps salt
- 2 ½ tbsp sugar
- 1 ½ tbsp gochugaru
- 1 tbsp of grated ginger
- 3 cloves of garlic, thinly sliced
- 1 tbsp each soy sauce and fish sauce
- 2 scallions, slivered
- 1 shallot, thinly sliced

Preparation

1. Toss cucumber spears with ½ tsp of the salt and ½ tbsp of the sugar. Leave them to macerate for about ten minutes.

2. Combine the remaining ingredients in a bowl, dissolving salt and sugar thoroughly and add drained cucumbers. Let this sit for at least 15 minutes before serving, but they will keep in the refrigerator for up to 2 weeks.

- Prep Time: 20 min. Brining Time: 1 day to 2 weeks
- Yields: 1 quart

Ingredients

- 1 pound scallions
- 4 tbsp gochugaru
- 4 tbsp fish sauce
- 2 tsps sugar
- 1 tsp grated ginger
- 2-3 minced cloves garlic

Preparation

1. Mix together all ingredients except scallions into a nice paste, then rub into cleaned and trimmed scallions (left whole).

2. Pack into a jar or place into a Ziploc bag and squeeze the air out. Leave to ferment at cool room temperature for 1 day, then refrigerate. It can be eaten immediately or stored for up to 3 weeks.

Kkaennip Kimchi (Perilla Leaf Kimchi)

Perilla leaf is related to Japanese shiso and a member of the mint family. It is used often in Korean and is worth seeking out at Asian markets during the summer months.

- Prep Time: 20 min.
- Brining Time: 3 hours to 3 weeks
- Yields: 1 ½ cups

Ingredients

- 50 Perilla leaves
- 2 tbsps gochugaru
- 1 tbsp each fish sauce and soy sauce
- 1 minced clove garlic
- 1 tsp sesame seeds, preferably toasted
- ½ cup water or vegetable broth or dashi (light seaweed broth)

Preparation

1. Be sure that perilla leaves are rinsed and dried well. Mix together remaining ingredients, then rub the paste into each individual leaf, stacking as you go.

3. When all leaves are coated, transfer to storage container, pour over any remaining spice mixture and seal. Leave out for 3 hours, then refrigerate and use within 3 weeks.

Jangajii

Jangajii is the general name for pickles in Korean. Unlike kimchis, these are not fermented. There are three basic methods for pickling in Korean cuisine, as explored below.

Soy Sauce Pickles

- Prep Time: 20 min. Total Time: 3 days
- Yield: 1 quart

Ingredients

- 1 pound Kirby cucumbers (small unwaxed cucumbers)
- 3 cups soy sauce
- 3 cups of sugar
- 3 cups of rice wine vinegar
- Garlic, chilis, scallions optional

Preparation

1. Bring soy sauce, sugar, and vinegar to a boil, then switch off heat and let it stand. Next, prepare the cucumbers.

2. Rub cucumbers with enough coarse salt to coat, massaging salt into the cucumber to scrub the peel and begin to make it malleable. Rinse, then pack into the jar(s) and cover with soy sauce mixture (you can leave cucumbers whole—these stay crisper for longer—or cut into thick rounds). Add any optional ingredients, roughly chopped, for flavor, if you like.

3. Let cucumbers sit out for 3 days, then refrigerate. These will last for a couple of months, growing stronger by the day.

This method works for all sorts of vegetables in roughly the same ratios, keeping soy to sugar to rice wine vinegar 1:1:1. Try a mix of whole garlic cloves and scallions; fresh green beans during the summer; or small boiling onions: experiment and enjoy!

Doenjang (Soybean) Pickles

- Prep Time: 15 min.
- Total Time: 1 week to 2 months
- Yield: 1 quart

Ingredients

- 1 lb. cucumbers, preferably English
- 1 cup doenjang (fermented soybean paste)
- ¼ cup of rice wine
- 1 tbsp sugar
- 1 tsp soy sauce

Preparation

1. Mix all ingredients together except for cucumbers. Scrub cucumbers well, then pack into the jar(s) and cover with doenjang mixture.

2. Refrigerate for at least 1 week before using and up to 2 months.

Like soy sauce pickles, this basic formula can be used for a wide variety of vegetables (green beans, radish, eggplant) and as a marinade for fish and meats (marinate skinless fish or chicken, cubed pork or beef overnight in the pickling mixture, then grill).

Brined Pickles

Truly, nothing could be simpler than traditional methods of Korean brined pickles. Simply use a ratio of water to salt at 10:1 (so, 10 cups of water needs 1 cup of salt). Bring brine to boil for about 5 minutes, cool slightly, pour over 2 pounds of vegetables while still hot. This won't cook the vegetables but will allow the brine to penetrate the flesh while maintaining crispness. Let stand at cool room temperature, weighted down, for 2 to 3 days, then pack into the jar(s), seal, and refrigerate for up to 1 month.

If a whitish film forms on the surface of brine, simply pour brine off, boil again for about 5 minutes before returning to the jar(s) and refrigerating.

Cucumbers are still the standard vegetable here but experiment with whatever is fresh and in season. Parboil sturdy vegetables like carrots when using this method.

Jjeotgal

Jjeotgal is the Korean term for "salted seafood." It can refer to a wide variety of condiments and side dishes, from its liquefied form (aekjeot: fish sauce) to pasty or chunky condiments that are served as part of the banchan (small dishes) of the Korean meal. The variety in Korean markets can be virtually endless in terms of the seafood used. Most forms of jjeotgal are purchased rather than made at home, but it can be done.

Essentially, clean and generously salt your choice of seafood, leaving it to cure for about six hours. Meanwhile, bring soy sauce, garlic, scallions, gochujang, ginger, and a bit of sugar to a boil (ratios depend on the amount of seafood, but about 2 cups of soy sauce to 1 pound of seafood with other ingredients included to taste). Pour while hot over salted seafood, then let stand for another hour. Drain and repeat this process another 5 or 6 times.

Soups & Stews

As detailed in <u>Chapter 1</u>, the geography and climate of Korea call for hearty, warming food. And what could better fit that need than delicious, often spicy soups and stews?

There are different categories of Korean soups and stews: **guk** and **tang** are thinner varieties, more like soup, while **jeongol** and **jjigae** are thicker, more like stews.

See below for recipes that will keep you cozy all winter long—and throughout the year!

Note on the stock*: homemade stocks are always better than canned.*

Korean cooking often uses a dried anchovy stock *which is very simple to make:*

1.   *boil a dozen plump dried anchovies in 6 cups of water for 10 minutes, then strain.*

2.   *Substitutions, such as chicken or vegetable stock, while less authentic, can be utilized.*

Kimchi KongnamulGuk (Kimchi & Bean Sprout Soup)

- Prep & Cooking Time: 30 minutes
- For 4 servings

Nutrition Info per serving

- Fat 1.1 g
- Carbohydrates 6.2 g
- Sodium1721 mg
- Calories 49

Ingredients

- 6 cups of stock
- 1 package bean sprouts (about 12 ounces)
- ½ cup cabbage kimchi
- ¼ cup liquid from kimchi
- 2 tsps fish sauce
- 2 minced cloves garlic

- 2 scallions, minced
- 1-2 tsps gochugaru (optional, for spicier results)

Preparation

1. Bring stock to a simmer. Rinse sprouts and chop kimchi into ½ inch pieces.

2. Add kimchi, kimchi liquid, and fish sauce to stock and lightly boil for 7-8 minutes until kimchi is almost tender.

3. Add bean sprouts and garlic and simmer for another 3 minutes. Toss in scallions and gochugaru, if using, and let flavors meld for a couple of minutes. Serve over rice.

Baechu Doengjang Guk (Cabbage Soup with Soybean Paste)

- Prep & Cooking Time: 30 min.
- For 4 servings

Nutrition Info per serving

- Calories 64
- Fat 1 g
- Carbohydrates 11.2 g
- Sodium1387 mg

Ingredients

- 4 cups stock (beef is also good here)
- 2 tbsp doenjang
- 1 tbsp soy sauce
- 1-2 tsps gochujang
- 1 head Napa cabbage
- 2 cloves garlic, minced
- 2 scallions, minced

Preparation

1. Start to simmer stock. Add doenjang, soy sauce, and gochujang to stock and whisk to make sure the ingredients are fully incorporated.

2. Cut cabbage into 2-inch pieces and add to stock. Simmer for about 15 minutes, until cabbage is done.

3. Toss in garlic and scallions and simmer for another 5-7 minutes.

Ganjaguk (Potato Soup)

- Prep & Cook Time: 40 min.
- Yield: 4 servings

Nutrition Info per serving

- Calories 233
- Fat 4.4 g
- Carbohydrates 32.8 g
- Sodium 154 mg

Ingredients

- 3 ounces of rice noodles
- 1/4 pound beef stew meat
- ½ tbsp soy sauce
- 2 cloves garlic, minced
- 3 medium potatoes
- ½ pound tofu
- 3 scallions

Preparation

1. For 20 minutes, soak rice noodles in lukewarm water, while preparing other ingredients.

2. Toss meat with soy sauce and garlic and let marinate while prepping remaining ingredients.
3. Peel and cut potatoes into ½ inch half moons. Cut tofu into slices of equal size. Cut scallions into 1-inch lengths.

4. Saute beef until browned, about 5 minutes, then put in 6 cups of water. Heat to a boil, then cover and simmer for 5 minutes.

5. Add potatoes and tofu, along with salt to taste, and cook potatoes until soft, about 5 minutes.

6. Add drained rice noodles and scallions and simmer for another 2 minutes. Serve hot.

Tteokguk (Rice Cake Soup)

- Prep & Cooking Time: 2 hours, mostly unattended
- For 4 servings

Nutrition Info per serving

- Calories 471
- Fat 5.3 g
- Carbohydrates 77g
- Sodium266 mg

Ingredients

- ½ pound beef, preferably brisket
- ½ white or yellow onion
- 6 cloves of garlic
- 3 scallions
- 1 tbsp (or more) soy sauce
- 1 tsp toasted sesame oil
- 4 cups sliced rice cake
- Sliced scallions and toasted nori (seaweed) for garnish

Preparation

1. Bring brisket, onion, garlic, scallions and 13 cups of lightly salted water to a boil in a large pot. Clear the surface of any foam that rises. Lower heat, cover, and simmer beef until tender, about 1 ½ hour.

2. Drain, reserving broth, and discard vegetables. Season broth with a tbsp of soy sauce. Shred beef into bite-size pieces and toss with a little bit of soy sauce and sesame oil. Reserve.

3. While beef is cooking or cooling, soak rice cakes in water to cover for about 20 minutes. Return seasoned broth to a boil and drop in drained rice cakes. Simmer for about 7 minutes.

4. Ladle broth and rice cakes into bowls and divide beef equally among each serving. Garnish with scallions and nori. This dish is often made at Korean New Year's celebrations.

Oi Naengguk (Cold Cucumber Soup)

- Prep & Cooking Time: 10 minutes
- For 4 servings

Nutrition Info per serving

- Calories 84
- Fat 1.4 g
- Carbohydrates 17.4 g
- Sodium 89 mg

Ingredients

- 3 Kirby cucumbers or 1 English cucumber
- 1 minced clove garlic
- 1 minced scallion
- 1 minced fresh red chili or 1 tsp gochugaru (optional, for a spicier version)
- 1 ½ tsps salt
- 1 tsp each sugar and soy sauce
- 2 tsps rice wine vinegar
- 1 cup water with 1 cup ice cubes
- 6 cherry tomatoes, quartered (optional)
- 2 tsps sesame seeds

Preparation

1. Cut cucumber into matchsticks and toss with garlic, scallion, chili (if using), salt, sugar, soy, and vinegar. Make sure salt and sugar are thoroughly dissolved. Let flavors meld for a couple of minutes.
2. Add water, ice cubes, and tomatoes (if using) and garnish with sesame seeds. Serve right away.

Dak Gomtang (Chicken Soup)

This is a very basic template for a bowl of Korean inflected chicken soup. It can certainly be customized with any number of additions: some gochujang for spice, or doenjang for funk; soaked rice noodles or cooked rice for heartiness; or cooked vegetables for freshness.

- Prep & Cooking Time: 2 hours, mostly unattended
- Yield: 6-8 servings

Nutrition Info per serving

- Calories 415
- Fat 15.6 g
- Carbohydrates 3.7 g
- Sodium 184 mg

Ingredients

- 1 whole chicken, 3-4 pounds
- 1 yellow onion
- 3 scallions
- 1-inch piece of ginger
- 1 tsp black peppercorns
- Chopped kimchi and sliced scallions, for garnish

Preparation

1. Put all ingredients in large pot, add 10-12 cups of water (enough to cover chicken), and bring to a boil. Clear the surface of any foam that rises.

2. Decrease heat and simmer, covered, for 45 minutes, until chicken is cooked through and tender. Drain, reserving broth and chicken. Discard vegetables.

3. Wait until chicken has cooled, then shred meat into small pieces, disposing of skin and bones.

4. Skim fat off broth if desired, then return chicken to broth (add any additional seasoning at this time, if you like). Serve over rice or noodles and top with kimchi and scallions.

Yukgaejang (Spicy Beef and Vegetable Soup)

- Prep & Cooking Time:2 hours, mostly unattended
- For4 servings

Nutrition Info per serving

- Calories 328
- Fat 14.4 g
- Carbohydrates 11.3 g
- Sodium 242 mg

Ingredients

- 1 pound beef brisket
- ½ white onion
- ½ pound daikon radish
- 3 whole cloves garlic
- ½ cup dried fernbrake (gosari, available at Asian markets)
- 3 dried or 6 fresh shitake mushrooms

- 1 cup bean sprouts
- 2 bundles scallions, coarsely chopped
- 2 tbsp toasted sesame oil
- 2 tbsp minced garlic
- 2 tbsp gochujang
- 2 tsps gochugaru
- 2 tsps soy sauce

Preparation

1. Put beef, onion, radish, and garlic cloves in the large pot. Cover with 14 cups of water and heat to a boil. Clear surface of any foam that rises. Lower to a simmer, top with lid, and cook until meat is falling apart about 1 ½ hours.

2. While meat is cooking, soak gosari and, if using, dried mushrooms for at least 30 minutes.

3. Drain meat, reserving broth, and when cool enough to handle, shred.

4. Toss shredded meat with soaked gosari, sliced mushrooms (fresh or soaked dried), bean sprouts, and scallions. Mix in minced garlic, sesame oil, gochujang, gochugaru, and soy. Return to broth and simmer for 10 minutes for flavors to meld. Adjust seasoning and serve hot.

Galbitang (Beef Short Rib Soup)

- Prep & Cook Time: 2 hours, some unattended
- Yield: 4 servings

Nutrition Info per serving

- Calories 1033
- Fat 82g
- Carbohydrates 28.7g
- Sodium566mg

Ingredients

- 3 pounds flanken cut (across the bone) short ribs
- 1 large daikon radish
- 1 white onion
- 3 whole scallions
- 5 cloves of garlic
- 3 thick slices of ginger
- 2 tbsp soy sauce
- 3 ounces sweet potato noodles
- 2 cloves garlic, minced
- 2 scallions, sliced
- Soy sauce, some pepper, and salt if you like

Preparation

1. Parboil the ribs: drop in a pot of boiling water for about 10 minutes, then drain and rinse. This step can be skipped but it removes impurities that might leach from the bones in the meat.

2. Cover ribs with 14 cups of water and add radish, onion, scallions, garlic, ginger, and soy. Simmer until meat is done about 1 ½ hours.

3. Remove radish from broth about 30 minutes into cooking, then chop into bite-sized pieces when cool enough to handle. Discard other vegetables.

4. Cover sweet potato noodles with water and soak for 30 minutes, then add to soup along with reserved radish and minced garlic. Cook for another 5 minutes or so for flavors to meld, and adjust seasonings. Served garnished with sliced scallions.

Haemul Jeongol (Seafood Hot Pot)

- Prep & Cooking Time:45 minutes
- For 4 servings

Nutrition Info per serving

- Calories 224
- Fat 3.7 g
- Carbohydrates 18 g
- Sodium 637 mg

Ingredients

- ¾ pound shrimp, deveined
- ¾ pound mussels, cleaned
- ½ cup sliced daikon radish
- 4 thinly sliced shiitake mushrooms, thinly sliced
- 1 small thinly sliced zucchini
- ½ cup bean sprouts
- 5 cups of water
- 1-ounce kombu (dried kelp)

For Sauce

- 2-3 Tbsp gochugaru
- 3 cloves garlic, minced
- 1 tbsp soy sauce
- 2 tbsp of rice wine
- ½ tbsp fish sauce

Tsp sugar

Preparation

1. Peel shrimp and reserve shells. Bring 5 cups water, cleaned mussels, and shrimp shells to a bowl in a large saucepan. Cover and cook until mussels just open, about 5-7 minutes. Strain, reserving broth and mussels. Discard shells.

2. Bring reserved broth back to boil and add kombu. Simmer for another 10 minutes, then remove and discard kombu.

3. Mix together sauce ingredients, ensure it is at the spice level you wish. Stir this into the broth and add radish. Cook for about 5 minutes, until radish, is tender.

4. Put everything left into the pot, bring the broth back to a hard simmer and serve as soon as seafood is cooked through about 5 minutes.

Bulgogi Jeongol (Beef Hot Pot)

- Prep & Cooking Time: 30 minutes plus overnight marinating
- For 4 servings

Nutrition Info per serving

- Calories 508
- Fat 12.9 g
- Carbohydrates 55 g
- Sodium 1522 mg

Ingredients

For marinade:

- 6 tbsp soy sauce
- 2 tbsp of rice wine
- 3 tbsp sugar
- 5 minced cloves garlic
- 1 Asian pear, peeled
- ½ white onion
- 1 tsp grated ginger
- Black pepper

For Hot Pot:

- ¾ pound beef, such as sirloin
- 4 ½ cups anchovy stock
- 5 ounces tofu, cut into small to medium squares
- ½ pound shitake mushrooms stemmed and thinly sliced
- 3 ounces sweet potato noodles, soaked in water for 20 minutes
- ¼ pound Napa cabbage, chopped into ½ inch pieces
- 2 scallions, sliced
- 1 red chili, sliced (optional)

Preparation

1. Blend all marinade ingredients in processor or blender. Slice beef paper thin (this is easier to do if you first freeze the meat for about 30 minutes, then slice) and toss with 1 cup of marinade. Marinate beef for at least 4 hours and up to overnight for best flavor. Reserve remaining marinade.

2. When ready to serve, mix stock with reserved marinade. Place beef in center of the large pot, arranging the rest of the prepared ingredients in small piles around it. Pour broth mixture over this and heat to a boil. Let bubble for about 10 minutes, serve over cooked rice.

Kimchi Jjigae (Kimchi Stew)

- Prep & Cook Time: 1 hour
- Yield: 4 servings

Nutrition Info per serving

- Calories 215
- Fat 14g
- Carbohydrates 5g
- Sodium 1002mg

Ingredients

- ¼ pound bacon
- 1 small onion, chopped
- 2 cups cabbage kimchi, chopped
- ½ cup kimchi liquid
- 2 tbsp gochugaru
- 1 tbsp gochujang
- ½ pound firm tofu, sliced
- 2 scallions, thinly sliced, for garnish

Preparation

1. Cut bacon into ¼ strips and cook over medium heat in a pot until browned, roughly 3 minutes. Pour off most of the fat, then add onion and soften it, roughly 5 minutes. Add chopped kimchi and liquid, turn heat to medium-high, and sizzle until kimchi softens and liquid evaporates, about 5 minutes.

2. Add gochugaru and gochujang, along with 2 cups of water. Cook at a simmer for 30 minutes.

3. Put tofu in the pan and cook for another 3-5 minutes, and serve stew garnished with scallions.

Haemul Sundubu Jjigae (Seafood and Tofu Stew)

- Prep & Cooking Time: 30 minutes
- For 4 servings

Nutrition Info per serving

- Calories 197
- Fat 7.9 g
- Carbohydrates 9.4 g
- Sodium 1061 mg

Ingredients

- 1 tbsp neutral oil
- ½ white onion, finely chopped
- 2 sliced scallions
- 2 minced cloves garlic
- ½ cup chopped cabbage kimchi
- ¼ cup kimchi liquid
- 3 tbsp gochugaru
- 3 tbsp soy sauce
- 14 ounces silken tofu
- 8 large shrimp, peeled
- ¼ pound squid, cut into rings
- 12 mussels, cleaned
- 1 large egg yolk (optional: egg will not be fully cooked)

Preparation

1. Heat oil over medium; add onion, scallion, and garlic. Soften everything for about 10 minutes. Add kimchi and liquid and saute for a little bit longer, about a minute.

2. Add gochugaru, soy, and 2 cups water. Heat to a simmer and cook until flavors come together, 5-6 minutes.

3. Put tofu in center of the pot, trying not to break it up, and encircle it with the seafood. Put the lid on and cook until mussels open, around 5 minutes.

4. Remove stew from burner and top with egg yolk, if using. Divide among bowls, breaking up yolk and tofu as you go.

Hobak Gochujang Jjigae (Spicy Zucchini Stew)

- Prep & Cooking Time: 30 minutes
- For 4 servings

Nutrition Info per serving

- Calories 154
- Fat 1.1g
- Carbohydrates 27.4 g
- Sodium 605 mg

Ingredients

- 2 medium zucchini
- 2 medium potatoes, peeled
- 2 tbsp gochujang
- 1 tbsp each of doenjang and soy sauce
- 3 green chilis, sliced
- 2 cloves garlic, minced
- 3 ounces ground pork or canned clams (optional: omit for vegetarian version)
- 2 scallions, sliced

Preparation

1. Cut zucchini into ½ inch pieces and potatoes into ¼ inch pieces.

2. Put 4 cups of water in a pot and stir in gochujang, doenjang, and soy. Heat to a boil and be sure ingredients are dissolved.

3. Add zucchini, potatoes and remaining ingredients except for scallions and simmer for 10 minutes, until potatoes yield.

4. Garnish with scallions and serve.

Budae Jjigae (Army Stew)

This is a peculiar stew, borne of a particular time in Korean history: the Korean War and its aftermath. The war brought American army bases and the processed foods needed to sustain soldiers with it; after the war, food was scarce in Korea and, thus, these American staples became a common way to make filling food. Be forewarned: while tasty, this stew packs a sodium punch!

- Prep & Cooking Time: 30 minutes
- For 4-6 servings

Nutrition Info per serving

- Calories 509
- Fat 11.4 g
- Carbohydrates 51.4 g
- Sodium 2343 mg

Ingredients

For sauce:

- 2 tbsp gochugaru
- 1/2 tbsp gochujang
- 3 cloves garlic, minced
- 1/2 tbsps sugar
- 2 tbsp of rice wine
- 1 Tbsp soy sauce

For stew:

- 4 cups stock (preferably chicken)
- 1 can SPAM, sliced
- 2 hot dogs, sliced on the diagonal
- ½ pound firm tofu, sliced ½ inch thick

- 1 pound shitake mushrooms, stems discarded and caps sliced
- ½ cup cabbage kimchi, chopped
- 1 package instant ramen noodles (discard flavoring packet if it comes with one)
- 2 ounces of rice cakes, sliced
- 2 scallions, sliced
- 2 slices American cheese

Preparation

1. Stir together all sauce ingredients.

2. Arrange SPAM, hot dogs, tofu, mushrooms, and kimchi in the pot. Place sauce in the middle. Pour broth over, cover pot, and heat to a boil. Then, lower to a simmer and cook for 5-7 minutes.

3. Add noodles, rice cakes, scallions, and cheese. Cover pot and simmer for another 3 minutes. Divide among bowls, serving over rice.

Saewoojuk (Shrimp and Rice Porridge)

- Prep & Cook Time:1 hr. plus 2 hrs.-overnight soaking
- Yield: 4 servings

Nutrition Info per serving

- Calories 284
- Fat 4.7 g
- Carbohydrates 41.8 g
- Sodium 491 mg

Ingredients

- 1 cup short-grained rice
- 1 tbsp neutral oil
- 2 minced cloves garlic
- ¼ cup carrot, diced
- ½ pound shrimp, peeled and chopped
- 1 tbsp fish sauce
- Sliced scallions and nori (seaweed), for garnish

Preparation

1. Wash rice in a few changes of water, swishing rice around until it looks clear. Drain a final time and add 4 cups of water to rice. Leave to soak for a minimum of 2 hours and up to overnight.

2. Heat oil over medium heat in a pot, saute garlic, carrot, and shrimp for a couple of minutes, coating with oil. Add soaked, drained rice and 7 cups of water to pot and heat to a boil. Cover, lower to a simmer, and let bubble away for 30 minutes.

3. Add fish sauce and salt to taste, then scoop into bowls, garnishing with scallions and nori.

Desserts: Hangwa and Tteok

Hangwa

Hangwa refers to traditional Korean confections in general. The following recipes are a sample of the different categories and a vast variety of Korean sweet finishes that are available to the serious home cook.

Dasik (Tea Cookies)

These cookies are simple, no-bake cookies, typically pressed into a mold especially for them. They are traditionally served at Lunar New Year festivities and are supposed to promote good health.

Green Tea Cookies

- Prep & Cook Time: 10 min.
- Yield: 1 serving

Nutrition Info per serving

- Calories 173
- Fat .4 g
- Carbohydrates 40 g
- Sodium 156 mg

Ingredients

- 3 tbsp rice flour
- 2 tsps powdered sugar
- Pinch of salt
- 1 tsp green tea powder (often called Matcha)
- 2 tsps light honey

Preparation

Mix all ingredients together, along with enough water to make a pliable dough. Press into dasik mold or roll into a thick sheet and cut with decorative cookie cutters. Multiply ingredients according to how many you wish to make of each kind.

Variation: Berry Tea Cookies

Use the same ingredients as above, substituting 2 ½ tsps prepared Omjia (Five Berry) tea in place of green tea powder and water.

These sweets are similar to American jello, with different and fresher fruit flavors and a typically firmer texture, though this is up to the cook. The method below is merely a suggestion: you can add more or less sugar and starch as you desire, as well as modifying the type of fruit and/or starch that you use.

- Prep & Cook Time: 20-30 min. plus 4 hours cooling
- Yield: 4 servings

Nutrition Info per serving

- Calories 190
- Fat 0g
- Carbohydrates 48 g
- Sodium 7 mg

Ingredients

- 1 cup fruit juice/puree, peeled and sieved if necessary (for example, Asian pear, persimmon, tangerine, grape, apple)
- ½ cup of sugar
- ½ cup starch (corn starch, potato starch, rice starch) mixed with 1 ounce water

Preparation

1. Prepare the fruit juice as necessary for the type of fruit and force through a sieve for a smoother texture. Mix well with sugar, sieve again to remove any potential lumps.

2. Stir starch into fruit and sugar mixture and heat to a soft boil. Boil for about 5 minutes, until mixture starts to thicken. Time will vary based on the kind of fruit and starch used.

3. Pour into a container or molds and let cool for 4 hours before cutting into pieces or turning out of molds.

Jeonggwa (Fruit Jerky)

This can be made with various fruits and vegetables, as well. Lotus root is popular. The following recipe uses beets, which are readily available.

- Prep & Cook Time: 1 ½ hour
- Yield: 18 pieces

Nutrition Info per serving

- Calories 200
- Fat 6 g
- Carbohydrates 37g
- Sodium 11 mg

Ingredients

- ½ cup peeled and grated beet
- 1 cup + 2 tbsp sugar
- 2 tbsp lemon juice (be sure to use fresh)
- ½ cup sesame seeds, preferably toasted

Preparation

1. Stir everything together, except seeds, in a heavy pot. Add a touch of salt and gently simmer over low heat, covered, for 40 minutes, stirring occasionally.

2. Remove lid and cook another 20 minutes, stirring frequently. It is done when the jelly drops from the spoon in lumps.

3. Meanwhile, place a sheet of parchment paper on countertop or cutting board and spread with half the sesame seeds. Carefully ladle the beet jelly on top of sesame seeds and sprinkle with another half of seeds.

4. Let cool for about 20 minutes, until still warm but cool enough to handle, and using parchment paper, shape into a log, about 8 inches by 1 ½ inch. Cut the jelly into pieces and serve immediately or wrap in cellophane to store.

Yaksik (Sweet Rice with Nuts and Fruit)

- Prep & Cooking Time: 45 minutes
- For 10 servings

Nutrition Info per serving

- Calories 201
- Fat 5.5g
- Carbohydrates 36 g
- Sodium 182 mg

Ingredients

- ¼ cup of sugar
- ¼ cup dark brown sugar
- 2 tbsps soy sauce
- 1 tbsp toasted sesame oil
- 2 tbsp neutral oil
- ½ tsp cinnamon
- 1 cup dried cranberries
- ¼ raisins
- ¼ cup honey
- 2 tbsp pine nuts
- 1 can water chestnuts, drained
- 4 cups cooked sticky rice

Preparation

1. Mix ¼ cup white sugar with ¼ cup water in a little pan and, over medium heat, cook until sugar caramelizes and becomes a dark brown color, about 8 minutes.

2. Mix together brown sugar, soy, both oils, and cinnamon in a large bowl, then add cooked rice and caramel. Stir together thoroughly.

3. Pack mixture into a steamer lined with cheesecloth and steam for 30 minutes.

4. Turn out into the pan to cool, where you can cut candy into squares or roll into balls.

Yugwa (Sweet Rice Crackers)

Traditionally, these are made from soaked glutinous rice flour in a days-long process. What follows is a handy simplification for the home cook.

- Prep & Cook Time: 35-40 min.
- Yield: 8 servings

Nutrition Info per serving

- Calories 394
- Fat .4 g
- Carbohydrates 95 g
- Sodium 3 mg

Ingredients

- 2 cups of sugar
- 3 thick slices ginger
- Neutral oil, for frying
- 1 pound tube-shaped rice cakes
- Sesame seeds

Preparation

1. Make sugar syrup by cooking 2 cups sugar with 1 ½ cups water. Add ginger slices to flavor. Cook over medium heat for about 10 minutes until thickened to a maple syrup consistency. Discard ginger slices.

2. Heat enough oil in large pan to fry rice cakes. Typically, these are twice-fried: first at a lower temperature to cook through and then at a higher temperature to brown and crisp. If frying twice, start in 275-degree oil, cooking cakes in batches of about 10 minutes each. Drain and cool slightly, then heat oil to 325 degrees and cook cakes again for a minute or two, turning to brown all sides. Transfer to paper towels or brown paper bag to drain.

3. Coat fried rice cakes in sugar syrup, then roll in sesame seeds.

Yumil-gwa (Fried Dough Sweet)

This is similar to the previous recipe, but with wheat dough and honey syrup.

- Prep & Cooking Time: 45 minutes
- For 10 servings

Nutrition Info per serving

- Calories 460
- Fat 13g
- Carbohydrates 85g
- Sodium4mg

Ingredients

- 2 cups plus 1/3 cup honey, divided
- 3 thick slices ginger
- 3 cups all-purpose flour
- 1/3 cup rice wine
- 1/3 cup toasted sesame oil

- ¼ cup finely ground pine nuts plus additional whole for garnish
- Neutral oil, for frying

Preparation

1. Put 2 cups honey and 2 cups water in small saucepan to make syrup. Add ginger slices. Cook at medium for 10 minutes, until thickened. Discard ginger slices.

2. Make the dough by mixing all remaining ingredients, including additional 1/3 cup honey, excepting whole nuts and oil. Roll dough into a rough square about 1/3 inch thick, cut into 2-3 inch cookies, using a cookie cutter or small glass.

3. Typically, these are twice-fried: first at a lower temperature to cook through and then at a higher temperature to brown and crisp. If frying twice, start in 275-degree oil, cooking cakes in batches for about 2-3 minutes a side. Drain and cool slightly, then heat oil to 325 degrees and cook cakes again for a minute or two, turning to brown all sides. Transfer to paper towels or brown paper bag to drain.

4. Toss cookies with honey syrup then sprinkle whole pine nuts over. You can also press whole nuts into the surface of the cookie while warm, making a design.

Kkultarae (King's Candy)

This is a deceptively simple recipe with tasty and fun results if you persevere. The end result should be somewhat like thicker, chewier cotton candy.

- Prep & Cook Time: 2 hours (includes cooling time)
- Yield: About a pound

Nutrition Info per serving

- Calories 295
- Fat 0 g
- Carbohydrates 77 g
- Sodium 1 mg

Ingredients

- 2 cups cornstarch
- 2 ½ cups sugar
- ¼ cup of corn syrup
- 2 tbsp of rice wine vinegar
- Food coloring, if you like

Preparation

1. Cook cornstarch over medium heat in a large pan for 10 minutes. Spread out on a baking sheet and reserve.
2. Bring corn syrup and sugar, vinegar, and ¾ cup water to a boil in a pot. Boil until mixture attains 250 degrees on a thermometer (a candy thermometer is best).

3. Pour into doughnut-shaped molds, preferably silicone, and chill in the refrigerator for an hour.

4. Pop candy out of molds, and roll in reserved cornstarch. Then, pull into string-like candy: with your hands, spread into a wide ring, twist to make a new ring, then pull again. Continue pulling and twisting to make longer and thinner threads of candy. Repeat.

Yeot-gangjeong (Sesame Candy)

- Prep & Cooking Time: 15 minutes
- For 4 servings

Nutrition Info per serving

- Calories 383
- Fat 26 g
- Carbohydrates 33.6 g
- Sodium 7 mg

Ingredients

- 3 tbsp honey
- 3 tbsp sugar
- 1 cup sesame seeds, toasted
- ¼ cup roasted, unsalted nuts (peanuts are traditional, but any nut you like will work)

Preparation

1. Bring honey, sugar, 1 tbsp water, and a touch of salt to boil. Boil for about 3 minutes, then stir in seeds and nuts.

2. Turn out onto parchment paper and shape with an oiled rolling pin into a ½ inch thick rectangle or square. Let cool slightly, then cut into shapes or squares with a sharp knife (dip knife in cold water between slicing to keep the mixture from sticking).

Tteok

Tteok is a category of sweets made of various kinds of rice cakes. They can be steamed, pounded, shaped, or pan-fried. See below for some recipes and methods for making tteok at home.

Steamed Tteok

Kongtteok (Bean tteok)

- Cook & Prep Time: 45 min. plus soak time
- Yield: 10 servings

Nutrition Info per serving

- Calories 372
- Fat 11 g
- Carbohydrates 55 g
- Sodium 21 mg

Ingredients

- 1 cup black soybeans
- 5 cups sweet rice flour
- 2 tbsp sugar
- ½ cup dried raisins or cranberries
- 1 cup walnuts

Preparation

1. Soak dried beans for 4 hours.

2. Mix defrosted sweet rice flour with sugar, breaking up any clumps. Stir in remaining ingredients, and place mixture in a steamer lined with cheesecloth. Steam for 30 minutes.

3. Wait until cool, then invert the rice cake onto a cutting board so you can slice into wedges.

Jeungpyeon (Rice wine tteok)

These are special occasion rice cakes for the harvest moon festival in Korea. Filled and shaped, often elaborately decorated, they are complicated to make. Below is a more accessible version for this tasty treat.

- Cook & Prep Time: 1 hr.
- Yield: 15 filled cakes

Nutrition Info per serving

- Calories 582
- Fat 13.4 g
- Carbohydrates 55 g
- Sodium 1 mg

Ingredients

- 3 cups sweet rice flour
- 3 tbsp honey
- 4 tbsp pine nuts, coarsely crushed
- 4 tbsp sesame seeds, toasted and coarsely crushed
- Pine needles, optional
- 1 tbsp toasted sesame oil

Preparation

1. Mix flour with ½ cup water and knead until smooth, around 2 minutes.

2. To make the filling, mix pine nuts with half of the honey in one small bowl; mix sesame seeds with half of the honey in another small bowl. Take 1 ounce of dough, roll into a ball, then make a well in the center and put in a tsp or two of filling. Shape ball around filling.

3. When all dough and filling have been used, place dough balls in a steamer lined with cheesecloth (and covered with pine needles, if using) and steam for 0 minutes. When done, remove to a serving tray and brush with sesame oil.

Baekseolgi (Raisin tteok)

- Cook & Prep Time: 40 min.
- Yield: 8 servings

Nutrition Info per serving

- Calories 506
- Fat 8 g
- Carbohydrates 85 g
- Sodium 2 mg

Ingredients

- 4 cups sweet rice flour
- ¼ cup of sugar
- 1-2 cups of dried fruits and sliced or chopped nuts (raisins, apricots, cranberries, almonds, pine nuts, walnuts)

Preparation

1. Put defrosted rice flour in a bowl and break up any lumps. Be sure it is fluffy then add sugar. Sift ingredients together.

2. Line a steamer basket with cheesecloth and place an 8-inch cake ring into the basket. Pack rice flour mixture into cake ring, then top with dried fruits and nuts.

3. Steam for 30 minutes then cool for a bit before lifting out of the steamer and removing cake ring. Serve immediately.

Pounded Tteok

Injeolmi (Sweet Beantteok)

- Cook & Prep Time: 15 min.
- Yield: 8-10 cakes

Nutrition Info per serving

- Calories 371
- Fat 2 g
- Carbohydrates 82 g
- Sodium 50 mg

Ingredients

- 1 cup sweet rice flour
- 1 tbsp sugar
- Pinch of salt
- ¾ cup of water
- ½ cup roasted soybean powder

Preparation

1. Mix rice flour, sugar, salt, and water in a microwave-safe bowl. Be sure to cover tightly with plastic wrap and microwave on for 3 minutes at high power. Stir ingredients again, then microwave again for 1 minute.

2. Put the hot dough into a mortar or other sturdy bowl and pound at least 50 times, about a minute or two, until the texture is chewy.

3. Form into 8-10 cakes, roll in roasted soybean powder. Add another sprinkle of sugar before serving, if you like.

Kkaeinjeolmi (Black Sesame tteok)

Follow recipe for <u>Injeolmi</u> above, substituting black sesame seeds for roasted soybean powder.

Danpatjuk (Sweet Bean & Rice Dumpling Soup)

- Prep & Cook Time: 1 ½ hr.
- Yield: 8 servings

Nutrition Info per serving

- Calories 347
- Fat 0 g
- Carbohydrates 78 g
- Sodium 319 mg

Ingredients

- 1 cup red beans
- 1-2 cups brown sugar, divided
- 1 tsp cinnamon
- 1 tsp salt
- 1 cup sweet rice flour
- Pine nuts, for garnish

Preparation

1. Cook red beans in water to cover until tender, about 1 hour. Drain and mash beans to a paste (or pulse them in a food processor). Mix bean paste with 1 cup of brown sugar, salt, and cinnamon. Set aside.

2. Make rice balls by mixing sweet rice flour with 1 tbsp sugar and add ½ cup of water to form a dough (add up to ½ cup more water if the mixture is dry). Form into ½ inch balls.

3. Put bean paste, 4 cups water, another ½ cup or more sugar and bring to a boil. Ladle in rice balls and cook until done around 10 minutes. Ladle into bowls and garnish with pine nuts.

Shaped Tteok

Songpyeon (Half-moon stuffed tteok)
- Prep & Cook Time: 2 hours
- Yield: 30 filled cakes

Nutrition Info per serving

- Calories 259
- Fat 3.2 g
- Carbohydrates 52.3 g
- Sodium 1 mg

Ingredients

- 2 pounds frozen rice flour, divided (optional)
- Water

For Filling:

- ½ cup sesame seeds
- 2 tbsp sugar
- 1 tbsp honey

Preparation

1. Most cooks will color their dough with natural dyes that also add a touch of flavor, such as blueberry juice, raspberry juice, or green tea powder. This can also be achieved with a few drops of food coloring, or it can be skipped altogether.

2. To make the dough, mix 2 cups rice flour with 4 tbsp liquid (water or juice), adding more liquid to form a shapeable dough. If making various colors, you should have enough to make 3 different colors in addition to plain. Let dough rest for 30 minutes.

3. Meanwhile, make filling: toast sesame seeds in a pan for roughly 5 minutes, taking care not to burn. Grind seeds finely, either in spice/coffee grinder or with mortar &pestle. Mix with sugar and honey.

4. Pinch off enough dough to make a 1-inch ball, make a well in the center, then add ½ tsp of filling, then shape dough around filling to make a half moon shape. Repeat with remaining dough and filling.

5. Line steamer basket with cheesecloth and steam filled cakes for 20 minutes. Don't allow cakes to touch each other; steam in batches if necessary.

Baram Tteok (Round stuffed tteok)

- Prep & Cook Time: 30 min.
- Yield: 16 balls

Ingredients

- 2 cups glutinous rice flour
- 7 tbsp sugar
- 1 tsp salt
- Food coloring, optional
- 1 ½ cup adzuki (red bean) paste: can be purchased at Asian markets or made at home; see danpatjuk recipe for directions)
- Cornstarch

Preparation

1. Mix rice flour, sugar, and salt with 1 cup water in microwave safe bowl (you can add food coloring here if you like). Microwave for 3 minutes on high power. Remove and stir for another 3 minutes, creating an elastic dough.

2. Divide red bean paste into 16 ping pong sized balls and set aside.

3. Divide dough into two equal portions and shape into long cylinders, then divide into 8 equal pieces each. Wrap dough around red bean balls and seal. Roll each in cornstarch.

Pan Fried Tteok

Hwajeon (Flower tteok)
- Prep & Cook Time: 30 min.
- Yield: 6 cakes

Ingredients

- Calories 169
- Fat 3.5 g
- Carbohydrates 33 g
- Sodium 0 mg

Ingredients

- 3 tbsp sugar
- ½ cup sweet rice flour
- 2 tsps neutral oil
- Edible flowers

Preparation

1. Mix 3 tbsp sugar with 3 tbsp water and cook over medium heat in a small saucepan until a syrup is formed about 5 minutes.

2. Mix sweet rice flour with a dash of salt and ¼ cup nearly boiling water. Knead the dough until it is smooth, then divide into 6 portions of equal size. Press each piece into a 2 inch round cake.

3. Heat oil in large pan (you don't want cakes touching). Fry cakes over low heat, in order to keep their white color, for about 4-5 minutes per side. When cooked through and slightly crispy, press an edible flower on top of the cake and flip gently, cooking for a few seconds to help the flour adhere to the cake. Serve immediately.

- Prep & Cook Time: 40 min.
- Yield: 4 servings

Ingredients

- 1 cup sweet rice flour
- 1/3 cup hot water
- 8 ounces red bean paste (available in some markets, or made from scratch as in danpatjuk recipe)
- 2 tbsp neutral oil
- 1 tbsp toasted sesame oil
- Pumpkin seeds, for garnish (optional)

Preparation

1. Mix 1 cup rice flour with water to make dough. If additional water needed, add. Knead for about 5 minutes, set aside to rest for 5-10 minutes.

2. Divide dough into 4 pieces of equal weight and roll each piece into a 5 inch round. Put 2 tbsp of red bean paste in the center, and fold dough over to create a crescent shape. Seal well.

3. Heat both oils in a large skillet and fry crescents 1-2 minutes a side. Press 2 or 3 pumpkin seeds in each crescent for garnish, if you like.

Drinks

Cha (Tea)

Tea is adored across the world, but perhaps no more so than in Asia. Korea has its own tea traditions and history, and Koreans happily make tea from any number of ingredients. See below for how to make three of the mostpopular types of tea drinks.

Green Tea: How to Brew

Method

Many people tend to brew the delicate green tea at higher temperatures than is advisable. For best results, steep 1 heaping tsp of loose green tea leaves in 1 cup of water warmed to 145 degrees. Steep for 4-5 minutes. Often, higher quality tea is steeped in minimally warmed water 2 or 3 times in order to bloom the delicate, complex flavor.

Barley Tea: How to Brew

Method

Koreans drink barley tea as a digestive aid, as well as for its uniquely nutty taste. Toast ¼ whole (not pearled) barley in a medium hot skillet for about 10 minutes. Meanwhile, bring about 1 quart of water to a boil. When barley is done toasting, add it to the water and lower heat. Bring to a bare simmer for 15 minutes, then strain. This tea is lovely served with a touch of honey to sweeten. This technique is also used with brown rice.

Fruit Teas: How to Brew

There are numerous fruit infusions, loosely categorized as teas, enjoyed throughout Korea and Asia in general. Brewing a fruit tea from fresh fruit is almost always superior to using "flavored" teas that you may find in the grocery store. Some of the most common in Korea are jujube tea, plum tea, and ginseng tea. These "teas" are not made with green or black tea, but as their names suggest are the brewed essences of the main ingredient. One very popular tea, Yuja cha (Citron tea) is often consumed to promote good health. See below for method.

Method

Scrub the peels of 5 citrons (yuzu) fruits and cut into thin slices, then quarter slices. Remove seeds but leave peel. Dissolve ¾ cup honey in a ¼ cup of nearly boiling water and stir. Add citron and crush fruit slightly to release flavors. Leave it to sit for a day, then refrigerate and use for tea: 1-2 tbsp citron marmalade per 1 cup hot water. If you cannot find fresh citrons, you can often find already prepared citron marmalade in Korean markets.

Cinnamon Tea

Method

Combine 8 sticks of cinnamon with 1 quart of water and ½ cup sugar. Heat to a boil, then lower heat and simmer for about 20 minutes. Fish out the cinnamon sticks and serve. This tea is often served cold, garnished with a spoonful of pine nuts.

Non-Alcoholic Drinks

Sujeonggwa (Cinnamon Ginger Punch)

Method:

Simmer about 20 cinnamon sticks in 11 cups of water for 40 minutes. In a separate pot, simmer 2 or 3 large pieces of ginger, peeled, in 11 cups of water for 40 minutes. Put 2 ½ cups sugar in another large pot, then strain cinnamon and ginger water into that and simmer until sugar is dissolved and flavors meld, about 20 minutes more. This is usually served cold, even slushy, garnished with dried fruits and nuts. Makes 20 servings.

Subak Hwachae (Watermelon Punch)

Method:

Ball or cube 4 cups watermelon (use a variety, if you like, of red and yellow watermelon or some honeydew for a visually stunning presentation). Using scraps from watermelons, puree enough to make about ½ cup juice, sieved if you like, and add to balls. Pour over 2 cups ginger ale, 2 cups strawberry milk, OR a mix of both to equal 2 cups. Stir in 3 tbsp mild vinegar or lime juice. Serve with ice cubes and a spoon to slurp up the watermelon. Garnish with other fresh fruit, such as pineapple and blueberry, if you like, and some fresh mint. Makes 4-5 servings.

Sikhye (Sweet Rice Drink)

Method:

Make barley tea, either following the above method or by using malted barley tea bags, often found in Asian grocery stores. You need about 8 ounces of tea bags to 15 cups of water (or, alternately, 15 cups of homemade barley tea). Place barley tea (or bags in water) in an oven safe dish; add 1 cup cooked short grain rice. Put in oven at its lowest setting for about 4 hours. Strain out bags, if using, and rice. Set rice aside. Heat steeped liquid with 1 cup of sugar until sugar is dissolved, then cool in refrigerator. Serve with a scoop of reserved rice and some toasted pine nuts. Makes 12 servings or more.

Alcoholic Drinks

Sul is the general name for alcoholic spirits in Korea. There are many categories, including rice wine (clear, milky, or flavored), distilled liquors such as soju, and beer. There is a traditional etiquette surrounding drinking in Korean culture, as well: be sure to pour for your elders and to receive a drink with both hands. Below are some traditional and not so traditional recipes for using Korean style spirits in your evening aperitif.

Soju Yogurt Cocktail

Method:

Soju, a grain spirit similar to vodka, lends itself well to a variety of cocktails. One popular in Korea is made with yogurt: for one drink, in a cocktail shaker, shake soju with 3 ounces prepared yogurt drink (such as lassi or kefir) and 3 ounces lemon-lime soda. To change it up, use a flavored yogurt drink and garnish with fresh fruit.

Soju is also sometimes mixed with cola, fruit juices, or tonic.

Flavored Liquors

Method:

Flavoring liquors or fermenting fruit from the vine is found the world around. Flavored liquors or wines can be found pre-made in establishments selling Korean spirits, but it can also be done at home. Pour a standard sized bottle of soju (750 milliliters) into a large container with a lid. Add ¼ sugar and about 1 cup of whatever fresh fruit you have on hand; let steep for at least two weeks, then strain. Popular fruits include citron (yuzu), raspberries, apples, and pears. Use what looks best! This method can also be used with rice wine, though reduce sugar to 2 tbsp.

Ginger Cocktail

Method:

While not traditional to Korean culture, both ginger and soju are prevalent in Korean cuisine. Ginger is thought to aid digestion, so this cocktail would make an excellent digestive. Make sugar syrup using ½ cup sugar, ½ cup water, and 3 or 4 slices of ginger: bring to a bare simmer in a saucepan for about 5 minutes, then cool and discard ginger slices. For one drink, mix 2-3 tbsps of ginger syrup, ½ cup soju, and squeeze of lemon or lime juice. Serve over ice, topped with a bit of sparkling soda water, if you like.

Conclusion

I hope you have enjoyed the vicarious experience of traveling through Korea. Often times, it is through food and a culinary tradition that one can get the best sense of a people and their culture. As the famous chef, Jean-Anthelme Brillat-Savarin reportedly noted, "Tell me what you eat, and I'll tell you who you are." We are lucky to live in a time in which we have access to a global pantry and a wide knowledge of various cuisines throughout the world. Korean food is a unique and hearty contribution to the world stage, a relative newcomer to the American market but a quickly growing standard.

Korean food is also healthy and vibrant, a break from the usual American meal, with its predominantly spicy and fermented flavors. With its emphasis on balance and in utilizing all five tastes, this kind of cooking is as intriguing as it is healthy—and, most recipes are quite simple to make at home, even without access to a specialty market.

The Korean meal is meant to be shared, family style, and brings people around the table to enjoy a meal together—a fading tradition that deserves a revival. With a pot of stew or a plate of grilled meat, some rice, kimchi, and a handful of banchan, you can explore a whole new world with your loved ones. Don't forget the tea and cakes!

Printed in Great
Britain
by Amazon